Augusta W Fletcher

The Other World and This

A Compendium of Spiritual Laws

Augusta W Fletcher

The Other World and This
A Compendium of Spiritual Laws

ISBN/EAN: 9783744666565

Printed in Europe, USA, Canada, Australia, Japan

Cover: Foto ©Thomas Meinert / pixelio.de

More available books at **www.hansebooks.com**

The Other World and This.

A Compendium of Spiritual Laws.

No. 1.
(COMPLETE.)

NEW WHITE CROSS LITERATURE.

The New White Cross Literature is a continuation of a similar line of thoughts presented to the public some time since, and is from the same source; the only difference being in the methods employed in their presentation. It is our purpose to continue the production of such works as will best represent our respective spheres of thought.

NEW YORK:
CHARLES B. REED, PUBLISHER,
164, 166 & 168 FULTON ST.

1893

INTRODUCTION.

The insufficient explanation offered for the various indications of a spiritual life, has led to a desire, on the part of every inquiring mind, to learn more of the hereafter, and of the action of the other life upon this.

Systems of theology have arisen, from time to time, played their part on the stage of life, and have, eventually, passed out of existence. That each has served its purpose for a time is admittedly true ; but a larger intelligence has demanded a more liberal religion, and, to-day, we stand amidst the crumbling walls of past opinions which are soon destined to mingle with the dust under our feet.

The mind of a man, in seeking to grapple with this problem of vital importance, has turned toward nature, and, through her mysterious workings, has found a partial solution, at least, of what has, for so long a time, enlisted his attention.

That some have found in the present phases of Spiritual Philosophy much that is comforting and true, will be admitted ; but we are inclined to go a step further and say that an arrangement of all of its laws, and the addition of many others, is necessary before a comprehensive idea can be given or received. Accordingly, we have taken upon ourselves the task of presenting, in simple language, such ideas as we feel will stand the test of logical reasoning, and have added thereto others which are the result of our experience in both worlds. It is impossible to separate the one world from the other ; so interblended are they in their interests and action, that in any work of this kind, a running analysis between the two is necessary for our meaning to be conveyed.

If we have leaned more toward any one phase of religious thought, it is because others have been so narrowed down by forms, and circumscribed by adherents, that they have eliminated the human elements through which the divine could be comprehended. In Spiritualism, however, humanity stands as a witness of God upon earth, and only through knowing mankind will it be possible to apprehend the infinite even in the smallest degree.

We have chosen the method for transmitting our thoughts that has best served our purpose, and we expect that the thoughts *alone* will be the subject of criticism. We do not hold that we have told the whole truth, or that we should be condemned because we have not. Jesus intimated to his followers that there were many things he had to say, but they were not prepared to hear them then; so there are many thoughts that crowd themselves upon our minds which we shall gladly give when there is a place for them in the world. Until then we shall content ourselves with giving such measure of truth as, in our judgment, the world demands, feeling that an honest thought was never uttered in vain.

Those of our readers who have been spiritually awakened will, we believe, find much in these pages that will commend itself; while those who are seeking the light may, perhaps, catch the crimson glow that precedes the dawning, and will press onward. There are many to whom our words will mean nothing; be that as it may, this effort is sent forth with the purpose, only, of awakening a realization of the infinite possibilities of man, and the destiny of the human soul.

AUTHOR.

CONTENTS.

	PAGE.
INTRODUCTION,	3
THE BODY, THE SPIRIT AND THE SOUL,	9
THE PHYSICAL AND SPIRITUAL NATURE,	17
THE SPIRIT AND ITS SPHERE OF ACTION,	25
THE AURA,	31
MENTAL STATES,	35
MENTAL OR SPIRITUAL SCIENCE,	43
MENTAL HEALERS,	49
CRIME BY INHERITANCE,	61
CONDITIONS PRODUCING CRIME,	65
IDIOCY,	69
INSANITY,	75
OBSESSION,	78
THE MYSTERY OF SLEEP,	85
DO WE TRAVEL WHEN WE SLEEP?	91
WHAT IS DEATH?	97
MODERN SPIRITUALISM,	113
DO SPIRITUALISTS BELIEVE IN GOD?	117
DO SPIRITUALISTS BELIEVE IN THE BIBLE?	118
DO SPIRITUALISTS BELIEVE IN THE DEVIL?	119
DO SPIRITUALISTS BELIEVE IN A SAVIOR?	120
DO SPIRITUALISTS BELIEVE IN HEAVEN AND HELL?	122

CONTENTS.

	PAGE.
Do Spiritualists Believe in Prayer?	123
Are There Evil Spirits?	124
Mediumship and Spiritual Phenomena,	129
Physical Mediums,	133
Trance Mediumship,	136
Healing Mediumship,	140
Inspirational Mediumship,	141
Materialization,	146
Remarks upon Mediumship,	153
Theosophy and Occultism,	163
Other Conditions in the Spiritual Life,	173
The Suicide's Story,	183
A Glimpse into the Spiritual World,	197
Some of the Subtle Laws of Life,	217
The Spiritual in Literature,	235
Has Man Lived More Lives Than One?	249
Suggestive Thoughts,	273

PART I.

THE BODY, THE SPIRIT AND THE SOUL.

THE BODY, THE SPIRIT AND THE SOUL.

(Entered according to Act of Congress, in the year 1893, by AUGUSTA W. FLETCHER, M. D.,
in the office of the Librarian of Congress at Washington.)

The body, sustaining, as it does, close relationship to the laws of physical life, is the external representation of man. It is so constructed that each part moves and acts in unison with each other part, all responsive to the common centre known as the spirit of man, but instead of the body acting of itself, it is, in reality, acted upon by the spirit, of which it is, in fact, the outer covering and to which it owes its existence.

The human body has, as a body, no intelligence, no activity, no purpose; but, when brought under the superior intelligence and controlling power of the indwelling spirit, it becomes all activity and directness of purpose. You know, then, the man, not through his physical body, *per se*, but through the action that his spirit (the spiritual man) makes upon that body.

The mind is the connecting link between the spirit and the human organism, as a window becomes a medium for transmitting light. The spirit is limited in its expression by the organism with which it is clothed; but its expression is seldom, if ever, the highest evidence of a man's spiritual life.

The soul is a direct emanation from the infinite, has never sinned, can never sin and must always be at oneness with the infinite spirit. It can never be embodied and knows not the limitations of time or space. It must remain in the realm of the unknowable and the consciousness of the individual must rest, to a greater or lesser degree, upon the assertion that it exists.

That there is something beyond the body is demonstrated by the existence of the spirit; that there is something beyond the spirit is realized by the unattainable, which forever floats before its vision and yet eludes its grasp. With soul and soul-life the individual has little to do beyond recognizing that there is a state of existence where the functions of life are not apparent, and where peace and happiness abound. These are the attributes of the soul, to which the individual spirit can never attain while there is a trace of selfishness, foolish ambition or unconquered desire remaining. That which is divine in man is alone found in the relation existing between the finite and the infinite soul. It can be justly said that the spirit is the expression which the soul makes in its contact with matter.

In giving a careful analysis of this subject we must not fail to recognize that each department of human life has its own desires, attractions and spheres of action. The body will often be at war with the spirit, so that the spirit will not reflect the pure light of the soul and, consequently, there will be great discord within the realms of the organization. The desires of the body which are perfectly legitimate in themselves, unless subjected to the wise direction of the spirit, are destined to lead to sorrow and regret; but those same desires, when they have received a higher impulse, may become the very foundation of a peaceful and happy life. To illustrate, a man may physically be so addicted to the use of intoxicating drink, and give himself up to the gratification of that appetite, as to waste his entire force in the excessive use thereof, while spiritually he abhors and repudiates the condition that is self-induced. Here we perceive the appetite of the body at war with the higher aspirations, and either the man will become a physical wreck, forever sinking lower in his downward course, or else well-nigh a fanatic upon the subject of total abstinence.

The spirit is enabled to but imperfectly manifest itself upon this plane of existence, and no one phase of human life, or perhaps a hundred, is sufficient to unfold its hidden possibilities.

There are two spiritual conditions which are apparent to every student of the spiritual nature of man, one called the lower, the other the higher. The former is responsive to the physical condition alone and, oftentimes, gains such strong sway over the individual as to completely obliterate the existence of the latter. The higher spiritual self is directly associated with the soul and is continually endeavoring to draw all beneath it to a still higher spiritual plane. In such natures, where the higher spiritual law rules, we have the philosopher, the reformer and the idealist, who, seemingly, are lost to the duties of time and sense and are swung out upon the ocean of such an universal love and law as to make them incomprehensible to the age and generation in which they live.

In developed natures, all the powers, both physical

and spiritual, play their respective parts under the wise direction of that superior intelligence which is manifested to every aspiring spirit. The body is the house in which the spirit lives; the spirit is the expression which the soul makes in its relation to matter.

Education or learning simply enlarges the sphere of action in which the spirit moves. Knowledge is one thing and education is quite another. Education is a growth gained through the study of books, wherein the ideas of others have been set down, and the spirit takes them up and gathers from them whatever stimulus and instruction they can convey. The powers of the mind are strengthened, the connection of the thought of others is made manifest and things far distant are brought near to view. The study of chemistry, astronomy, geology, or any of the various branches of natural science, is valuable only in what it suggests to the mind of the student. The possession of knowledge without a comprehension of its use is of comparatively little value, and the present system of the education of the young is most unwise and ill-considered. Far too much time is worse than wasted in the study of dead languages, which convey no meaning to the modern mind, and various other branches of study which never come within the sphere of the individual necessities. Still, the unfolding of the mind and the developing of the individual capacities prepares new avenues through which the indwelling spirit may reveal itself.

There is an education, however, far above and beyond anything that books contain or teachers impart, and that is individual knowledge born from close observation and direct personal experience. Man is never able to understand fully any emotion or condition until he has passed through it himself and, when that has been done, his own individual apprehension of it and its meaning will produce a deeper impression upon his spirit and life than that same experience ten times repeated in the lives of as many others; for at best, when others are passing through a trying ordeal, the effect which it produces can only be observed and that most imperfectly, since natures differ so widely one from the other. Sorrow that expresses itself in lamentations, tears and sighs is the soonest susceptible of consolation, seems to breathe itself out and, after a time, to be wellnigh forgotten; while the grief which is of so deep a character that it fails to find any outward expression is, by far, more abiding in its nature and, perhaps, far more real. And yet, the one who makes the most noise, the greatest outward showing as to the effect that the sorrow has produced, is bound to receive the most sympathy from the looker on, while the other is, not infrequently, condemned as being hard-hearted simply because no sign is made. It is not that you are appealed to by any outward thing that you show a sympathetic spirit, but rather through a sense of the interior life of another which links you with him to that extent that that which is his becomes yours. And what is true of sorrow is equally true of joy. If possession was thought less of and the spirit of beauty recognized more universally, there would be far more happiness and enjoyment in the world than there is to-day. But, through innate selfishness, man has grown to feel that he must first possess and then enjoy, and the struggle he has to make in order to accomplish the first step, often incapacitates him for the taking of the second.

Suffering may be sympathized with by the superficial observer, but he who suffers or has suffered and learned the lesson, can alone understand its meaning. Any of the phases of experience in life has more to do with rounding out and developing the spirit than all the education found in books that can be crowded into the human brain in a lifetime.

PART II.

THE PHYSICAL AND SPIRITUAL NATURE.
THE SPIRIT AND ITS SPHERE OF ACTION.

THE PHYSICAL AND SPIRITUAL NATURE.

(Entered according to Act of Congress, in the year 1893, by AUGUSTA W. FLETCHER, M. D.,
in the office of the Librarian of Congress at Wash'ngton.)

The human body has been justly called the temple of the living God; realizing that, the more perfect that temple the more complete will be the expression of whatever power there is within and beyond it. Health is to the body what happiness is to the spirit, and we might say that health and happiness walk hand in hand together.

The body is dual in its nature: two hands, two eyes, two ears, two lungs, each one able to perform a part of the necessary work of life, yet both necessary for its complete fulfillment. It is as if there was an individualized spirit in each of these different powers, which has a distinctive sphere of action. The hands can never do the work of the eyes, nor the feet accomplish the purposes of the lungs, but by the united action of all of these different members, the human body becomes the important factor which it is upon the earthly plane of existence. The nerves of the body extend throughout every one of its various members and are only so many lines of telegraphic communication which convey the will and desire of that intelligent self which gives an entity to the individual.

Food, clothing and suitable surroundings as to light and heat are the essential requirements of the body itself, and serve as a protection against any foreign element or power. Should an accident occur, whereby any member of the body is affected, such as the breaking of a leg or arm, or the putting out of an eye, the telegraphic connection has simply been cut off, and, unless it should be re-established, such member would live or remain as extraneous to the body politic itself. In any surgical operation whereby these members are removed, the consciousness of the individual will sustain no loss, nor will it ever recognize spiritually that such an operation has taken place, although physically he may suffer much inconvenience therefrom.

In our acquaintance a man had the misfortune to be injured in a railway accident and, after much suffering and pain, both legs were amputated just above the knee, and, being placed in a box, were subsequently buried in the ground. Shortly after the operation the patient complained bitterly of suffering from great pain across the top of his feet, and was gradually losing strength in consequence of it. In vain the physician and attendants tried to persuade him that he had no feet and that consequently his sufferings were purely imaginary, but as the days wore on his complainings increased and his life was despaired of. Finally a physician, who had made nervous diseases a specialty, was called in. After questioning the patient carefully and observing the symptoms, he left the sick-room, and inquired what had been done with the limbs after amputation, and was told that they had been placed in a box and buried in an adjacent field. He accordingly visited the spot, had the box taken up and found that the lid was pressing firmly across the top of both feet. He had the lid removed, placed the members in a proper position, nailed up the box and reburied it. Then he revisited the sick-room, where he found the patient quietly sleeping, and in a short time he speedily recovered, never complaining afterward of suffering further pain in that direction.

This illustration goes to show that there is a close connection between every member of the body and the centre of intelligence, and that when those members are severed the connection does not always cease to exist. And again, it shows that for every physical member of the body there is a spiritual counterpart and while the one may be lost, the other still remains, although invisible to the external eye.

Physical disease is due to the introduction of some element foreign to the body itself, and is usually taken on when the body is exposed to some extraordinary condition with which it is not in accord, or to the lack of positive nerve power, which lack renders the body too weak and sensitive to expel any foreign element that may be thus unconsciously introduced. We may be allowed to say, since relations between the body and the spirit are so closely allied, that if the spirit was kept in positive activity and the nerves thereby supplied with all the vitality that could be appropriated, physical disease would be a thing unknown. It is the lack of this supply, the lack of complete responsiveness of the body to the spirit, that renders disease possible and its cure so difficult.

The laws of heredity, as relating to physical bodies,

are made to play a too important part in the question of disease. It is true that each human being inherits certain physical elements from his parents, and that disease is not unfrequently transmitted from one generation to another, but the continuance of this disease in later life is by no means arbitrary, and is possible of elimination by a process which will be referred to later on under the head of "SPIRITUAL HEALING," since it is the purpose of this article to refer to physical conditions only, and the introduction of other matters relating thereto might produce confusion in the mind of the reader.

In the process of years the body undergoes a large number of changes, due to a variety of causes too numerous to mention. Modern science has demonstrated that this same body passes through such changes that at the end of one year not a particle of the original body remains. If this be true, it will be readily seen that under wise direction even the law of heredity can be controverted. If the body is constituted of elements more or less diseased, it will be possible to place said body in relationship with healthy elements, and thereby replace one by another. In fact, every year death is taking place, and yet, the death of each element is anticipated by the birth of a new one. How easy then to fill the place of the element that is thrown off by one of renewed life and vitality.

St. Paul said, "I die daily." He might have added, "I am born daily," with equal truth. It is upon this law of careful chemical adjustment that the physical health and death of the human race depends. When that law is fully recognized and practiced, disease will be a thing unknown, and the death of the body dependent upon the desire of the spirit, instead of physical disease.

We cannot leave this subject without also referring to the matter of food and physical surroundings, to which we might, in fact, devote the entire space of this volume with profit.

More persons suffer from excess in eating and drinking than from any other one cause. Drunkenness—or better say over-drinking—is an evil that has wound itself around the very vitals of civilization, breathing forth destruction and misery wherever its poisonous coils are felt. Homes are wrecked, lives ruined and ambitions sacrificed upon the altar of this appetite; and yet the evil results from over-eating, though less plainly manifested, are, by far, greater and more universal. The needs of the body are one thing, its desires another; it is always right in its demands and never makes a mistake. But when the appetite, developed to abnormality, begins to assert itself, destruction is bound to follow in the footsteps of its gratification. A simple diet which produces neither stimulation nor excitement should be to the body what fuel is in the fire-box in a steam-engine, and is bound to result in making the body what it has always been destined to be, namely, the simple instrument in the hands of the spirit. The more prominent the appetites, of whatever nature or character, the less prominent the spirit. Use your appetites as the foundation of greater achievements and all will work together for good; abuse them by every gratification and disease and destruction are destined to follow. The idea of a purely vegetable diet, or living solely upon fruits, which in the future may be accepted as a higher form of life, at the present time, with the labors imposed upon the ordinary individual, would not be conducive to the best results. However, the tendency of the age is toward the spiritualization of material things and great changes have been made, even in the matter of diet, during the past century. It must be remembered that not only what you eat, but how you eat it, produces an effect physical as well as spiritual.

Food taken amidst the confusion of inharmonious magnetic conditions will never produce a satisfactory result. The quantity of food swallowed hurriedly in a railway restaurant, in the midst of a crowd of people bent upon laying away as large an amount as is possible in a given time while the train waits, does not produce one-half the strengthening results as a much less quantity would under more favorable conditions. During the time devoted to eating, no matter how simple the fare, any disagreeable or annoying topic should be laid aside and such pleasant themes of conversation introduced as will leave the mind in an inactive state, and render the body receptive to all the surrounding magnetic conditions. Never sit at the table and partake of food in company with an enemy or any persons who may entertain unkindly feeling toward you. Better partake of no meal at all and leave the system to recuperate itself from an hour's quiet rest, than be charged and surcharged by the poisonous emanations which discordant natures are bound to throw off and which are taken on as the food enters the system.

External surroundings have much to do with the normal condition of the physical body. The present form of civilization herds together thousands in a space that can poorly accommodate as many hundreds. Crowded together are men and women of totally different temperaments who are bound to have a more or less deleterious effect upon each other. Working, eating and sleeping are so commingled with foreign influences, due to over-crowding, that nothing but the poorest results as to work and life can rightfully be expected. Every city, instead of spending large sums of money in the beauty and magnificence of its public buildings and monuments, would serve the present age and posterity to greater purpose if the same amount was used in forming numerous public squares which would serve as a breathing-place for the people and an escape for the poisonous gases and influences that are consequent upon life in all the large centres of civilization. God would be better served in the one day set apart for the recognition of His supreme power by a studying of His works as seen in the green fields and wooded slopes of the country than listening to the oftentimes stupid expositions of narrow-minded theologians. Fresh air, the breath of God, and sunshine, the smile of God, are far more important factors in the religion of life than all the arguments upon infant damnation and eternal punishment.

In short, we can condense our thought upon how to take proper care of the body in these words:

Be cleanly; be active; be natural; live as much as possible in the open air; let as much sunshine into your homes as you can; govern your appetites by the needs of your body, and never forget that rest is as essential as activity. By rest we do not mean idling or simply killing time, which, in many instances, frustrates the very purpose that is sought. Rest is often found through a complete change of employment by calling into activity other powers of the mind, while those most frequently in use are, for the time being, laid aside. Thus the mind, weary with books, may find much that is restful in music or, again, a man immured in business may leave the Stock Exchange behind him and, seeking the mountains or the seashore, find a source of strength through a complete change; but, if he sits down and folds his hands to wait until the Summer is past in order to return to take up the work he has left unfinished, he will find himself at the end of his vacation worse than he was at the beginning. On the other hand, if he cultivates different forms of amusement, drops his dignity for the moment and goes at pleasure with the purpose of getting everything out of it that he can, he will find, on his return, that he has enlarged his world, strengthened his system and gathered together an amount of nerve force which will materially affect the results of the months that are to follow.

THE SPIRIT AND ITS SPHERE OF ACTION.

(Entered according to Act of Congress, in the year 1893, by AUGUSTA W. FLETCHER, M. D.,
In the office of the Librarian of Congress at Washington.)

Large and important as the body may appear in its sphere of action, it is as a drop of water to the ocean in comparison with the vast realms that are unfolded for the activity of the spirit. In fact, the material universe and the human body are in themselves but one phase of spiritual existence. It might be said the lowest phase, since spirit, *per se*, knows of no temptations save when brought in contact or relationship with some lower element.

It is not our purpose, however, to speak of the activity of the spirit as a spirit in spheres where, freed from earthly environments, it is enabled to work out its destiny, but rather to consider the action of the spirit in connection with the human body, and to indicate such laws as may more fully enable each individual to accomplish his highest destiny. That that destiny is some time to be accomplished, all will admit, and the more that is crowded into one life, the more rapid is the advancement along the pathway of progress.

Spirit stands first, and the human organism is but the result of its action. From the moment of conception to the hour of death, the spirit is allied with physical conditions and is continually making a supreme effort to reveal and express itself through them. To hold that the physical environments with which a spirit clothes itself are all-sufficient for a complete realization of itself would be to do away with the object and purpose of life altogether. The very incompleteness and insufficiency of these aforesaid environments furnish an object to be accomplished.

From those realizations, out of which a possible life is generated, there is at once established a magnet of attraction for the spirit, and the months of gestation are necessary to more firmly assert and affix that attraction. This is not always accomplished, and in such cases death ensues even before birth. Such deaths are usually attributed to accident or disease, which is really only a part of the true cause, since it is to these occurrences that the breaking of the aforesaid magnetic conditions may be due. If, however, the development proceeds uninterruptedly and the birth takes place, the spirit immediately, with the first breath of life, assumes complete control of the body and thus the career of life is begun.

During the first fifteen years impressions are very easily made, and the spirit readily takes up conditions which, in later life, when its individuality has become more strongly asserted, it as readily repudiates. During these years the child is kept well and happy to the degree that it is allowed to live a natural life, but the continual talking about disease places it in relationship with that thought and it becomes almost at once susceptible to it. At the age stated, the spirit assumes a higher control over the organism and begins through this to attract magnetic influences to itself. Heretofore, it has not been able to hold its own, and this explains why the health of children is so affected by being brought in contact with persons much older than themselves; the magnetic centre not being established until the change from childhood to manhood. After that time, influences of all kinds are attracted to the indwelling spirit.

It must be understood that there are no mistakes in the realms of creation, that everything that lives lives for a purpose, whether that object be comprehended or not; every desire of the spirit being for a purpose, and the object of life is to wisely select for fulfilment such intimations as will result in the greatest good. It has been wrongly assumed that to be natural every desire of the spirit must be expressed. Were it not so, a condition bordering upon chaos would be the result. Selfishness would be rampant and the impulses would assume an authority which would materially interfere with the progress of the individual. Many claiming to be natural are nothing more or less than impertinent and ill-bred and assume naturalness as an excuse for expressions which no person of ordinary courtesy would indulge in.

One has not to be unkind simply because he differs from another, nor are adverse criticisms, when intelligently expressed, to be looked upon as evidences, necessarily, of either ill-temper or jealousy, and only a small mind would so consider them. There are, however, almost as few people who are prepared to receive intelligent criticism as there are those who are capable of giving it, consequently, it becomes every wise man to consider both actions and words before they are launched upon the sea of activity. While they are unexpressed, they belong to the individual; when once they are brought into action they become the property of the world. There are as many desires given for repression as for expression. A grape-vine left to follow out its own inclination will bear numberless clusters of imperfect fruit. The wise gardener nips off one-half, if not two-thirds, of them and when the harvest time comes presents you with less quantity, but a perfected quality, of the same. Take this illustration to mind, for upon its understanding much of your success and happiness depends.

PART III.

THE AURA.

MENTAL STATES.

THE AURA.

(Entered according to Act of Congress, in the year 1898, by Augusta W. Fletcher, M. D., in the office of the Librarian of Congress at Washington.)

It will be readily recognized that every individual is surrounded by an unseen influence which partakes, more or less, of the characteristics of his personality. You never take the hand of a friend, or enemy, for that matter, without receiving a series of sensations not explainable from any given cause. You feel an influence that either attracts or repels you, and this is due not to the words that may be spoken, nor the manner of greeting, but from the assimilation of the unseen influences that surround you both. This imperceptible something which either may attract or repel is vaguely called magnetism, and oftentimes serves a greater purpose than either character or mental attainments.

An influence of this kind pervades all bodies, but is particularly noticeable and is susceptible of a degree of analysis in the human. In other words, every human being is surrounded by a sphere of influence which extends from the head to the feet. To the clairvoyant it is apparent, differing in color and intensity according to the moral and physical condition of the individual. A person who lives in the atmosphere of study and has sacrificed his health to advancement in this direction, will be surrounded by an aura that appears to be yellow in color; another who is of a sympathetic nature will be surrounded by an aura blue in color, while a third who lives a purely physical life is seen to be red in color. Wherever there be two or three distinctive traits in the individual there will be as many colors represented. If the individual be affected by disease the aura is intercepted by dark shadows.

This aura is finer than ether itself; is chemically composed of life-giving elements and is used by all magnetic and mental healers through a direct exercise of the will. It is, however, only through the perfect blending of one aura with another that any good result is attained, and what is called attraction and repulsion, as instanced through individuals meeting each other, is dependent upon the affinity or non-affinity of this element.

Persons at a distance may intelligently admire and appreciate each other, and, while removed by space, may remain steadfast friends for many years, but when they come together, discord may be the result, due to the fact that while they are spiritually allied to each other they are magnetically opposed.

Many marriages are nothing more or less than magnetic attractions, which, when the attraction has ceased, culminate in disgust and regret. In fact, great care should be taken in not associating too continually with each other, no matter how great the liking or affection, for the two spheres are bound, under the varying emotions and conditions of life, to irritate each other, and what otherwise might be a joy and a blessing becomes an annoyance.

Distinctively magnetic healers are those who are surrounded by a strong aura which they are able to impart through general association, without any particular mental effort whatever. They employ the laying on of hands or manipulation to accentuate the imparting of this influence and, through this process, are more readily able to obtain a result ; but after a treatment of this kind the patient and the operator should separate at once, for if the operator remains any length of time he is bound to attract all of his influence back again, leaving the patient weary and depleted. But though the healer has given to the sufferer a part of himself which the system very readily appropriates, it is well to say here that no person not in perfect health, and over fifty years of age, has any right to act in the capacity of a magnetic healer and, again, that no such person should be employed for whom the least repugnance or unpleasantness is felt.

In cases where all influences are equal and there is a complete sympathy between the operator and the patient, the best results can be assured. The remedy depends wholly upon the law of adaptability and unless the law of harmony can be established, more harm than good will eventuate from the effort. The lack of understanding in this regard will account for the numberless failures that have brought healing, in this direction, into disrepute. No person is capable of obtaining good results for every patient, and the sooner the healer recognizes this most important fact and begins to classify the line of patients he is capable of treating with success, the better. Young children are especially susceptible to the magnetic aura surrounding those with whom they are brought in contact and are not infrequently punished for giving expression to a repulsion which their elders are not able to understand or appreciate. And what is looked upon as perverseness is, in many cases, but the action of the law of repulsion which, asserting itself, should be recognized rather than condemned. Animals, also, have a strong magnetism, frequently more invigorating than that of human beings, since it is less vitiated by lawless and unseemly living. Dogs and horses are most noticeable for their strong magnetic influence, while cats and birds possess an influence often deleterious in its effects.

MENTAL STATES.

(Entered according to Act of Congress, in the year 1893, by AUGUSTA W. FLETCHER, M. D., in the office of the Librarian of Congress at Washington.)

What are known as mental states are really conditions in which the spirit finds itself. Selfishness is a purely physical condition reflecting itself upon the spirit and, oftentimes, to such a degree as to almost bury it. A selfish person thinks only of his individual gratification and is disturbed only so far as such gratification is interfered with either by persons or circumstances.

It is not infrequently said of a man "what an agreeable friend he would be if he was not so inordinately selfish." A person of this character is immured in such intense physical environments, usually the result of heredity, as to interfere with the action of the spirit altogether. It is a mistake, however, to gratify any such propensity and, no matter what the cost of friendship or feeling, it should be firmly and strenuously opposed. Selfish people are given to expressions of great violence and temper, which is another evidence of an undeveloped spiritual state and is the cause of many of the phases of nervous disease. It is useless to argue with an angry person; in fact, it is much wiser to leave them at the point where argument becomes a necessity. Quiet and reflection will do more for such an one than all the arguments in the world. Pacific measures, under all circumstances, when dealing with minds equipoised, or even partially so, effect the best results. In this way a double power is gained, for much mental strength is retained and any loss of nervous or vital force prevented.

Love is a distinctively spiritual element and finds its expression in kindness, charity and sympathetic feeling. But there is no word so commonly used and so little understood as is this one. Self-love is only another name and form of selfishness; but love, pure and simple, combines, within itself, principles of justice and equity coupled with a desire to please and encourage. One is the antithesis of the other, and the more in harmony the spirit is with itself the more strengthening are the emanations and impressions received therefrom. The law of love and the law of happiness are other words for the same thing. Under the sway of this condition, no matter what the physical environments may be, they are made secondary to the higher purposes.

Thus you will perceive some persons surrounded by poverty, lying for years upon a bed of illness, with the outer world, in fact, shut out; yet there will be an interior happiness perceptible that will light up the dullest places and seemingly raise the sufferer far above all physical pain. This is especially exemplified in the case of the blind, who are compelled to live a purely interior life and who, after a time, so enter into the realms of the ideal that they rarely feel much loss at what the world calls a great misfortune. Give the spirit free scope to act and the best of results are destined to follow; but this is seldom done, and whenever spirit-needs are sacrificed to the desires of the body illness and discord are bound to follow.

We admit the existence of disease, which we term the introduction of elements foreign to the sphere of the individual, and suggest, as a remedy, the following:

In the case of purely nervous diseases there is nothing that will serve to readjust the nervous system so quickly as to bring the patient into relationship with such harmonious individuals as will, by reflection, produce the same effect in himself. If disease, in all its departments, be more or less contagious, health is equally so. By associating with a diseased person continually you will, after a time, become similarly affected. Being in the atmosphere of a healthy and harmonious nature is bound to produce a like result also, so that despondent natures, thus affected by nervous irritability and haunted by dark forebodings, can be remedied far more by sunshine and happiness than by narcotics and drugs. The spirit really knows what it wants, and if it is in a state of apparent suffering it is due to its not being able to establish the magnetic connections whereby those influences can be attracted.

In purely physical disease the mind, recognizing the physical deformity, serves to intensify it by continually thinking about it, since the thought conveys strength to the pain. If you are suffering and every one remarks how pale you look and, with a pitying expression of countenance, commiserates in mistaken sympathy, you allow this condition to interfere with all your work and duties and it increases in intensity as time goes on; but if you are thrown into pleasant company, your attention or interest enlisted, the pain is forgotten altogether. Or, again, should you have the toothache, the pain being severe, you go to your dentist and ring the bell, determined to have the offending member removed. Suddenly, you find it has ceased to ache because of the greater pain you anticipated in having it extracted. Now, if the tooth is absolutely affected, it were worse than folly to endeavor to combat that condition; but, up to the point where it is disturbed, although remaining in a healthy state, it is possible, by an effort of the will, to eliminate the pain. And this is true of every other form of physical suffering.

The mind, so called, has the power not only to create pain, but to increase and intensify it. Four-fifths of the diseases with which mankind is afflicted are purely imaginary. That is to say, they exist mentally and are produced by mental reflection.

"I am afraid I shall take cold" renders the person susceptible to that condition. He has laid the foundation for that result and made himself amenable to it. Thinking of evils is an invitation for them to visit you, and they rarely come singly.

It is our effort to impress upon your mind that when in health your spirit is, firstly, in harmony with itself, and secondly, in harmony with the physical body in which it is placed. In disease, it is out of harmony with itself and out of harmonious relationship with the body; *ergo*, the successful physician is one who establishes the harmonious condition of the spirit first and then deals with the effect that its inharmonious expressions have made. We have not here alluded to what is an important factor in the health and happiness of the individual, namely, the influence that one spirit may have over another and, when we say the spirit, we are speaking of the embodied rather than the disembodied. This influence may be of the most dangerous character; can never be guarded against too carefully and its result can rarely ever be foretold.

The imperfect understanding of hypnotism, mesmerism and psychology renders individuals in their present state of development victims to influences which they cannot see externally and can only realize in effect. Waves of hate and discord may be sent out from a point and they will affect all of those who are in a state to receive such an influence. In fact, it is very difficult for the undeveloped person to separate his own state from the reflected states that are cast upon him, and thus an incentive, and a very great one, is found for the study of spiritual science.

Murders have been perpetrated by individuals who are absolutely irresponsible, just by the concentration of given minds upon a certain point. It is not necessary that they should concentrate upon an individual, but upon a thought, and any individual who is in the line of that thought-wave is bound to take it up and act upon it.

The South hated Abraham Lincoln to a man and felt that if he should die their cause would be won. Wilkes Booth was a strangely emotional person with southern sympathies. The South dwelt upon this thought until it rolled like a mighty wave over the land. Booth was just in that state where he caught the influence of it and carried out its purpose. He was hypnotically responsive to that thought-wave.

Hypnotism in the hands of the good and the wise is a power for great good, in the hands of the ignorant and vicious a means of great harm.

It is a law in nature that, whether spiritual or material, like attracts like. If you desire the worst, place yourself in a low condition and you will attract it; if you desire the best, place yourself in a high condition and by determined effort you will attract that also. But it must be remembered that so-called evil is more readily attracted than so-called good, inasmuch as the human being is upon the earthly plane of existence where undeveloped conditions are more rampant than their opposite.

PART IV.

MENTAL OR SPIRITUAL SCIENCE.
MENTAL HEALERS.

MENTAL OR SPIRITUAL SCIENCE.

(Entered according to Act of Congress, in the year 1893, by AUGUSTA W. FLETCHER, M. D., in the office of the Librarian of Congress at Washington.)

There arises a great difference in the discussion of mental science as to the relative meaning of terms, and, without doubt, a vast amount of the disagreements existing among many advanced thinkers is the result more of the use of terms than in the meaning itself. The term mental science does not express what it should, but we are compelled to employ the word "mental" in preference to the word "spiritual," since the former conveys a more distinctive meaning than the latter. Justly speaking, it should be "spiritual science" instead of "mental science," for reasons which the following will explain:

Mental science has demonstrated the existence of a world in which thoughts become realities and dominate all external evidences of human life. Heretofore, the investigations of modern science have been confined to what is called the discovery of nature's laws, but nature has been limited to only such conditions as were susceptible to measurement and visibility, and it has been the position taken by the most prominent scientific men of the present day, that that which cannot be demonstrated to the external senses does not exist. To be sure, the apparent presence of mind is recognized, but it is accepted as a result of physical causes rather than being the direct agent itself and ceases to exist when the elements that constitute the human organization cease to attract and act upon each other.

Mental science, however, reverses this order of things and insists that external results are governed by internal causes and that mind stands first, while all external forms are the result of its action. If there be any apparent disturbance in the human organism the cause must be looked for and will, no doubt, be found in the mental condition of the sufferer. In effecting a change, then, the mind must first be brought into harmonious relationship with itself and then with each representative member of the body.

The physician who carries with him a fund of good nature and kindly influence and has the power of imparting both, will accomplish more good in the sick-room than the wisest professor of medical science that you could introduce there. This idea, however, does not discountenance the use of medicine in some cases where the mental state has become so deranged as to produce an absolutely physical disturbance; but it does relegate medicine, and the practice of it, to a secondary place.

And what is true of the action of the mind over the body is equally true of the action of the mind over all bodies. That the connection which the human mind sustains to the body, in which it is encased and connected to, is much higher than that which it is able to exert over foreign bodies is admitted, but that is due, in part, to the greater harmony existing between the body and the mind and its long association. There is a law of harmony existing between all bodies and all minds, and the effort is to establish harmonious relationship with this law. This being done any purpose can be accomplished.

A musical instrument of inferior make will do better service to the hand accustomed to manipulate it than a finer instrument used for the first time. The carpenter, the tailor and the artist accomplish better results with the things directly associated with them in their work than they can with tools with which they are not acquainted. The clothes you wear become a part of yourself, since there is a personal magnetism which permeates all things directly brought in contact with you, and becomes as much a part of yourself, and susceptible to your own mental emanations, as is the body in which you live.

It is the object of mental science to reveal the other side of nature, to point out the soul of nature, which is made visible now only through external demonstration.

The practice of mental science is not confined to any one sphere of action, since every department of life is governed and controlled from one centre of action, and by one and the same power. It depends upon the direction given to the force as to what the result will be. The sphere of mental science has been popularly considered to relate to the physical and mental condition of the individual; and the exercise of mental power is accepted as a remedial agency. It is, in fact, a superior condition of the mind that is enabled to dominate an inferior condition of the body and to subjugate any lower states, into which the physical organism may drift, to the will of the superior mind. For it must be remembered that there are both superior and inferior mental states. The superior state is the one in which selfish enjoyments are merged into the law of universal good, while the inferior states relate to the transitory indulgencies. But the same force that, by a proper exercise of its possibilities, can eliminate and conquer any inharmonious physical condition can also be directed toward any other material object, such as the accomplishment of specific purposes, the direction of purely worldly enterprises and the attainment of any purpose which may result in ultimate good. That is to say, in the laws of mental science, a man may become a power among men, may influence and direct them either for good or evil as his own individual development and desire may indicate. He may take these same laws into his business and become a power therein for the carrying out, successfully, of great business enterprises; or, again, he may become a shining light to those who are in the darkness, by revealing how each may become a law unto himself. And how is that done? First, the individual must recognize that all men are equal only in possibilities, not in present form of development; that the lowest is equal to the highest only when he has developed that which is highest within himself. Inequality must ever exist wherever there is a difference in the manifestation of human attributes. Then the mind is recognized as the master and the body as the servant. The true object of life is to bring both into such perfect and harmonious relationship as to serve the highest good.

The art of thinking is one but little understood, and upon this art all success in the realm of mental science depends. Few individuals are able to finish one thought before it is intercepted by the action of another. Thus they lack directness of purpose and are continually wasting their power over half-fulfilled plans. The man to work, successfully, must be able to give the entire force of his nature to any single purpose that he may have in mind, and the ultimate result will depend upon his ability to do so. Do one thing at a time and to that give all your force. Strength of will is simply the devoting of all the energies of the mind to the given purposes.

The men regarded as strongly individualized are each governed, either consciously or unconsciously, by this rule. Any work that is worth doing at all is worth putting one's entire self into. Life should be so divided as not to permit one interest to invade itself upon another. In the hours of business, foreign interests should not be allowed to intrude themselves; and the hours of pleasure should not be crowded by the demands of business. A careful observance of this law will give to business undertakings a stronger force, to the hours of pleasure an added sweetness, and to the life a satisfactory completeness unknown to those whose mental states are continually disturbed by every passing thought.

The complete concentration of the mind upon any given purpose is the secret of success. It must not be understood that this condition can be attained at once, or by a single effort, or that simply wishing for a thing means concentrating upon it. Mental concentration is only attained in its complete sense after long and severe trial. Every person can approximate unto the law of mental science and, by the study thereof, attain a degree of mental enfoldment. But there are comparatively few, in this stage of the development of the human race, who are able to practice it with any great degree of success. It is well to think before you act, rather than to act and think afterward; to have in mind what you wish to accomplish and, forgetting everything else, exert yourself to that end.

Each person requires a certain part of every day to himself when he shall disconnect himself from the members of his own household even, and, if it be for not more than five minutes, pass that time in self-examination and quiet. It is not the number of things that are attempted, it is those things that are well done, that constitute the importance and value of life.

Mental Healers.

(Entered according to Act of Congress, in the year 1898, by AUGUSTA W. FLETCHER, M. D., in the office of the Librarian of Congress at Washington.)

Mental healers differ largely from magnetic healers in much the same way that homœopathy differs from allopathy. It is not so much the quantity of the influence that is imparted, but the intensity of it, that produces a satisfactory result.

The mental healer has an aura which, by effort of the will, he sends to a given point and is enabled to expel a certain amount of influence from his own sphere, which, in turn, finds a resting-place in the surroundings of the patient. Distance offers little or no impediment.

The hypnotist is one who uses this power for amusement, but precisely in the same way. For example, an operator wishes to hypnotize a number of persons; he bids them concentrate their minds upon a given point and then grasps them firmly so as to produce some slight physical pain which shall attract their attention. As the eyes are turned from that point to him he catches their mind, so to speak, and they are instantly drawn into the magnetic sphere of his presence and while there they experience whatever emotions he may desire, never realizing, even afterward, that they have been acting otherwise than they desired themselves, and not infrequently in direct opposition to their own natural inclinations. Many times persons greatly averse to intemperance and having a horror for anything low and offensive, have been known to deliver a powerful lecture upon the virtues of intemperance and to indulge in language that was coarse and revolting.

A surgical operation has recently come under our notice where the patient was put in a magnetic sleep by the will of the operator in order that a limb might be amputated without pain, and this was successfully done without any show of suffering whatever. Just before the patient was thoroughly awakened the operator, in handling the instrument carelessly, cut himself, and the subject, who had remained perfectly quiet during his own operation, cried with pain when the operator met with the accident and ever after, when the operation was referred to, declared that he felt nothing save the cut on his hand which, in reality, he had never experienced.

The mental healer has a wider range of activity than has the hypnotist; but his methods are bound to be similar. We do not wish to cast any reflection either upon hypnotic or mental scientists, for we are aware that there is little love lost between them. We are simply recording facts as they exist.

The mental scientist, to cure his patient, must lift him by sheer force of will out of the sphere of disease into which conditions have thrown him, into his own more harmonious and helpful one. There may be different means suggested by the occasion for the accomplishment of this end, but this is the result that must be obtained in the counteracting of untoward conditions.

The blood and its circulation is one of the conditions upon which physical health absolutely depends and its action should be carefully watched so as to get the circulation in as normal a condition as possible. The brain, the heart and the base of the spine are the three great centres from which the system derives activity and strength.

The brain is more closely allied with the spirit than are the other two centres and, should it be surcharged with blood, will intensify the nerve supply throughout the system, producing nervous excitation and hysteria. Consequently, the attention of the healer should be directed upon the lower extremities, thereby attracting the blood from the brain and thus equalizing its distribution throughout the system. The breathing comes next in importance and, if careful attention is also paid to this, it will serve to strengthen the patient and counteract opposing effects.

Many persons breathe superficially; that is to say, the upper lobe of the lungs alone are used while the lower lobes are left in a state of comparative inactivity. Frequency of breathing vitiates and depletes the system, but, by breathing deeply, the entire lungs are filled and cannot fail to become strengthened and invigorated. This should be carefully observed in children, but the advice is quite as pertinent to adults. There are chemical changes resulting from deep breathing that act upon the entire system which the lungs, in a superficial breathing, never undergo and even those who are in perfect health should devote, at least, a few moments during the day to its practice. Throw the shoulders backward, place the feet together and stand with your back against the side of the room. Count while the inhalation is made, repeating the same numerals while the breath is held and, again, recount while the breath is exhaled. At first a sensation of giddiness about the head and heart will be felt, but if this be persisted in, the beneficial result will be almost incalculable. In incipient consumption it is sure to be attended with success, since it will force the depleted lung cells to act in spite of themselves. Exercise—and by that word we mean the general activity of the body—is conducive to the best results if not overdone.

There is a magnetism in the atmosphere as palpable as is the aura in individuals, and this cannot fail to benefit most persons when not taken in too great excess. The reason why most persons experience so much benefit from an ocean voyage, is that the magnetic lines of their surroundings are cut off there. It is on the water or on the mountain tops that the purest magnetism is found. The sermons that Jesus preached were delivered from the mountain top, where the atmosphere was not impregnated by the cross currents emanating from selfish minds. He could never have preached in the market-place as he did on the mountains. Whenever he wished to gain inspiration he went into the wilderness and found it through fasting and solitude. He thereby reduced the physical ascendency of the body, which food is ever bound to induce and, through disassociation from all earthly minds, rendered his spirit receptive to the higher thoughts that alone are found in the realms of the spirit.

Your patient, then, will recover physical and spiritual equilibrium far more quickly through living in the country, being thereby removed from the distractions of intense civilization. He will not feel as well at first, for this difference in magnetism is, for the time, too stimulating, and induces an abnormal state. But after awhile he will find his own magnetic level and begin to exist in a more natural way.

We do not wish it to be understood, however, by what has been said, that the patient should be absented from all society or deprived of pleasant and sympathetic association; but that the varying influences of individuals who are bent upon getting rather than giving is to be discountenanced, while in their place two or three others, who are magnetically as much in sympathy as their particular organizations will permit, should be placed in close relationship with him.

It will be seen from the above that the healer cannot do everything although, sometimes, he may think so. He, at most, can but assist his patient in getting into closer relationship with the laws of health and, when these are established, he must do the rest of the work himself. Thus it will be to a great degree self-cure, which, in fact, is the only permanent one.

Under another head we have already spoken of the subject of diet, which should play as important a part as does exercise itself. It is the quality of food rather than the quantity which produces a healthful result. If we have spoken from the physical side alone, it has been because such hints, which are too frequently ignored by the healer, may be of great assistance.

We leave it to the intelligence of those who practice in this line as to the amount of diversion and amusement the patient may require. Remembering, always, that whatever the mind is occupied with, or however exciting the moments are, effects may be produced which are better than to allow the patient to be continually dwelling upon himself.

We propose to give a few examples which may, at least, be of benefit to the operator, wherein both the mental and physical are combined. Drunkenness, opium-eating and other habits that produce a deleterious effect, are the first which suggest themselves. The drunkard, through excessive use of liquors, has introduced certain chemicals into the system which are continually crying out for their counterpart. If the entire effect of a drunken debauch could be expunged from the system directly after its conclusion, the appetite would not become the overpowering one that it is; but with these chemicals remaining in the system, they are constantly being added to and, after a short time, so preponderate that the individual feels that he cannot live without a certain amount of alcoholic stimulation. The brain becomes excited and, up to a certain time, is more the instrument of the spirit than when in its normal state. But the boundary line between this condition and its opposite is all too quickly passed. In treating a man for drunkenness, this chemical condition must be taken largely into consideration, for the individual who is thus afflicted is as much under the hypnotic influence of alcoholic chemicals as is the subject under the sway of the operator. The Keeley cure and other such inventions recognize this physical effect in a somewhat limited way at present, but they are working in the right direction. They introduce into the blood certain chemicals which counteract the other elements in the system and, at the same time, do all they can to encourage the patient both mentally and spiritually.

The mental healer will be compelled to work in precisely the same way, only if he be strong in magnetic possession he will be able, by the effort of his own will, to impart the essence of these counteracting chemicals in the magnetic wave which he will project upon the patient. But he will require to be in somewhat constant association with the patient so as to hold his mentality within his own grasp. In such treatment both patient and operator should, for the first weeks, take frequent baths to remove the elements thrown off and constantly exercise in the open air, while, at the same time, liquor should be present on the sideboard so that the patient will not receive the impression that he is governed by any outside will.

And what is true of liquor and its excessive use, relates with equal pertinence to the use of all narcotizing drugs. We have known morphine patients, who have been greatly addicted to its use, to be perfectly satisfied with a hypodermic of hot water, believing all the time that it contained the much-loved drug. But a gradual reduction of the supply is, after this has been followed for a week say, not attended with permanent results. The enormity of the habit is lost sight of and the patient, seeing no ill effect from a moderate indulgence in these drugs, at once begins to rest upon what he is pleased to call the *Use* of them. After the first week, close the door absolutely to the habit and then work both materially and spiritually to expel the poisonous elements, which die only from starvation.

Crime is another dark shadow that hangs over the fair face of present and past civilization. Various means have been devised as the remedy for and control of its expression. Criminal propensities are almost universally the result either of inheritance or are due to a negativity of the spirit, whereby its possibility is not properly unfolded, nor individual control attended to. Murderers, and their kind, are almost always possessed of highly excitable temperaments and, though they may execute their designs with great clear-headedness, yet there will always be some underlying grievance which inspires it. Crime is a disease and as such should be treated by the sympathetic heart rather than punished by an obdurate judge. What personal deformity is to the body, the tendency of crime and the thirst for blood are to the spirit. Jails and prisons may deal with the physical side of the question, but an intelligent mind will see how superficial such treatment is. Of course, the whole thing springs from improper generation and can never be wholly rectified until as much care, at least, is given to the creation of human beings, as the florist or the breeder of cattle is compelled to devote to perfection in his especial line.

Children, for the most part, HAPPEN to be born. The temperaments of the parents and the best conditions that should surround their conception and generation are things rarely ever considered, and those who, with indifferent spirit, take upon themselves the responsibility of becoming parents should not, in turn, be wholly relieved of the consequences of their action.

This is a question that must enlist, to a much greater degree than it has thus far done, not only the attention of the physician and the reformer, but also that of every intelligent human being. These matters cannot be left to take care of themselves and then society punish the result as a means of protecting it from unjust invasion, but the underlying causes should be dragged out into the light, carefully analyzed and the conclusion arrived at, therefrom, entered upon the lawbooks of the world. It is not enough that every restraining influence which a humane government can devise is exerted for the unfortunate and afflicted for their benefit, since the same amount of strong effort and attention would, in a short time, prevent the constant accession of numbers to this class. Surely, every boy and girl should be taught the laws governing their physical and spiritual life; should be made to feel that the responsibilities accruing from their exercise should rest with them, and that every child has a right, if the best is to be expected of him in the future, to be born under healthy conditions and in happy surroundings, not as a result of indiscretion or excess, but as a crowning glory of a union of both hearts and hands. It is a fact that these important questions are not discussable in spheres polite, are really looked upon as altogether too delicate for the ordinary mind to consider, and that ignorance in regard to them is both excusable and commendatory, while those who violate the law most are seemingly oblivious to any responsibility whatever, and persistently go on their way regretting the mistakes made through ignorance, the while silencing the voice that is raised in protest against it, forgetting that the only way out of all this present chaos will alone be found through meeting the difficulties squarely and discussing them intelligently. More important than the condition of man after death, is a knowledge of the laws upon which his life depends before birth; for, if he be born rightly, the future will take care of itself, and the part now played by religion and theology in the drama of human life will be wholly an unnecessary one, for the child will be so much in accord with himself and, consequently, in harmony with God, as to render the necessity for regeneration and redemption entirely out of question. He will know no fear as to the future life, for, being guided by the never-failing light within, he will walk in that straight path that leadeth unto greater light, where all goodness and truth abide.

PART V.

CRIME BY INHERITANCE.
CONDITIONS PRODUCING CRIME.
IDIOCY.

CRIME BY INHERITANCE.

(Entered according to Act of Congress, in the year 1893, by AUGUSTA W. FLETCHER, M. D.,
in the office of the Librarian of Congress at Washington.)

It would appear that the law of heredity finds an illustration in the case of children who, from the earliest years, seem to have a desire to do wrong. Generally, the parent, in anger for the wrong committed, punishes the child, developing by reflection the same spirit of anger in the culprit. At once the child would, in turn, inflict like punishment upon the parent if he could, but the superior physical strength of the former wins in the fight and the child, though conquered, is not convinced. And the system of legal punishment is based upon the same plan and, while this is so, most criminals leave the jails, prisons and reformatories where they have been serving out their sentences, in a worse state than when they began. In fact, these institutions can, with great show of truth, be called schools of crime and cesspools of vice. What the young criminal does not know, through lack of proper classification among the prisoners, he learns from the old offenders.

There have been many children guilty of murder, boy-murderers they are called, for whose action this law of heredity, or the presence of some invisible influence not recognized by the general mind, will furnish the only explanation. We have observed such cases as that of Jesse Pomeroy and find that, through the occupation of his father, he inherited the thirst for blood which developed itself in all the horrible atrocity of the crime he committed. Allowing the right of such persons as his parents to marry and have children, there should be a better solution to the result of such a marriage than a lifetime in the penitentiary.

And what is that solution? The moment that the tendencies of the child became apparent, and their baneful effect recognized, he should have immediately become the subject for the attention of the physician and, if this state could not be counteracted, removed from associations where danger was likely to occur, instead of waiting for the intervention of the police. That is to say, he should have been surrounded by influences of an exactly opposite nature and have been taught to control his temper; and, in fact, the whole mental state changed, which could have been readily done through the administering of proper magnetic influences.

We hear the objector say that all this would entail great expense of time and money upon society. If that be true, so long as society recognizes a violation of nature's laws, it should bear such expense, no matter how great it may be. The time will come, it is not far distant, when, instead of the criminal being always a criminal, crime will be recognized as a disease resulting from the transgression of nature's law, and it will be the object of those who understand this law to pity, instead of condemn, and to strengthen, rather than punish, those who are thus afflicted. Today, the moment a man passes the portals of the prison in which he is condemned to serve a given number of years he finds himself in another world, out of which all the sunshine and human sympathy has been taken, and he is made to feel that he has dropped below the level of the lowest who are within, and becomes joined to a class against whom the hand of the world has ever been and will ever be lifted. Instinctively, a rebellion against fate is raised within him and, although he may be able to recognize the justice of his punishment for the crime committed, he will find it difficult to escape the greater penalty which society and the world impose, and which continues long after the law, itself, has been satisfied. The stamp of Cain is upon his brow, and go where he may, and strive with all the effort of his power, the words "he has been in jail" will be sufficient to close the doors of the most humane against him. Years of repentance, tears and prayers are all insufficient to wipe out the stain.

The criminal imperceptibly recognizes this fact and, instead of growing from crime and aspiring to higher and better things, which the after-years shall realize, he passes his time of punishment either in cursing his enemies or evolving new schemes in which there will be less danger of being discovered than formerly. But he gradually becomes less and less susceptible to every benign influence; he hardens his heart against every tender suggestion or thought and finally goes forth more at war with society than, in turn, society is at enmity with him. Cruel as were the influences of the prison, they are more than intensified by the treatment he receives from the world when he comes out, and thus all that is good is crushed out of him and all that is evil is strengthened. When this is recognized, a system will be evolved whereby penitentiaries will become places of reformation indeed and the theologian, who plays such an unimportant part in the world, confining his attention to the events expected to occur some time in eternity, will find this sphere of usefulness of more account and value.

We have not referred to the punishment of criminals by death, whether it be upon the gallows or by the more modern invention of electrocution, for such punishment is fast passing away, to take its place among the other relics of barbarism which a higher civilization has already repudiated. It is well, however, to observe that the apparent effects produced by these legalized murders are most alarming in their result.

Conditions Producing Crime.

(Entered according to Act of Congress, in the year 1893, by AUGUSTA W. FLETCHER, M. D., in the office of the Librarian of Congress at Washington.)

The larger part of the great army of criminals is not stamped by the law of heredity or any distinct propensity for wrong-doing, but they are possessed of the elements which, under wrong direction, may develop in most adverse ways. The half-formed physical organization, over which the spirit has but an incomplete sway, is subject to passing influences that, for the time, completely prevents any spiritual impressions of a higher order and, oftentimes, draws the man into the mire of destruction and death.

Physiology and the much-laughed-at claim of phrenology serve to illustrate that, when a great crime is committed, there is something wrong with the individual, physically, and this disease—for whatever is wrong in the system cannot be called by a better name—prevents any direct action of the higher self. Many a criminal has found it difficult to understand why he committed a crime, as have his fellows who had no part or connection with it.

The general tendency of the human body is like unto that of less developed animals, and you would hardly hold an animal responsible for acting out its nature. The lion and the tiger feed upon human beings, and individuals, brought into the realms of civilization, are so placed that they cannot carry out the original instincts of the body except by violation of laws framed to meet social conditions. Human beings, in some instances, where the physical largely predominates, are scarcely more responsible than animals and, when under the sway of their angry passions, which they have never been taught to control, become the victims of invisible influences which carry them along the swift current of their own evil intents.

In recruiting men for the army, or for any responsible position where physical strength is required, the state carefully examines into their condition and, in many cases, into the antecedents of the applicants as well, so that they will be able to perform the duties of the office which they are about to accept.

The time will come when, in the study of the development of the human race, this line of examination will be applied to every department of life and physicians will be wise enough to discover criminal tendencies and place those who are afflicted under such benign influences that a remedy will be assured. That this will entail more hospitals for a time is true, but there will be less jails and prisons.

Some years ago, when leprosy was common throughout Palestine and, through commingling and lack of cleanliness, was becoming almost epidemic, Dr. and Mrs. Valentine foresaw a great work that might be accomplished not only for these unfortunates themselves, but for the community in which they lived. To cure the disease or even remedy it was a recognized impossibility, so an institution was built outside the walls of Jerusalem, through generous contributions, and persons thus afflicted, or any one who had symptoms of disease, were gathered in with the hope of preventing them from contaminating others with their contact and thereby stopping its increase by confining it to the individuals alone. That is to say, those afflicted should live apart from their fellows and with their death the germs of the disease would die also.

It is our idea that those who are afflicted with the symptoms of crime should be dealt with in precisely the same way, and that the highest laws of society should be employed in either remedying or eliminating evil tendencies in their incipiency, rather than in punishing the criminal afterward. This alone could be done by absenting the patient from the friction and heat of everyday life, with an impulse to develop the higher and the better side of the nature which, in every instance, is possible.

It will be readily understood that soil left to itself never produces a harvest of either fruit or grain. It runs away to weeds, oftentimes of a poisonous nature. It remains for man to cultivate the soil, root out the weeds and plant the seed for the harvest in their place. Man, to-day, is an undeveloped soil running to weeds; indeed, the careful training of the wise hand and then the implanting of seeds which shall give new impulses and higher purposes to the human mind is required. We have said all this with the idea of leading up to the one point, namely, that the mental healer is probably the only one who can accomplish much good in the premises indicated. He will perceive by our argument, which, from the nature of the subject, is bound to be somewhat discursive, that in the criminal or the man of criminal tendencies, the lower self predominates to the exclusion of the higher self, and that his province is to take such afflicted persons out of the realms of moral and spiritual darkness and bring them into the fuller light of the truth, always being willing to accept whatever material aids the development of medical science has to offer.

But punishment is neither a remedy nor a preventative in the true sense. Legislation, no matter how severe the enactments, will never be able to circumvent the mental activities of evil-disposed minds. It requires this law of higher education; it requires that individual responsibility shall be taught even to the child, and more than that, every human being should be made to feel that he is honest and true for honesty's and truth's sake, because they are best, rather than through fear of the penitentiary or the gallows.

IDIOCY.

(Entered according to Act of Congress, in the year 1893, by AUGUSTA W. FLETCHER, M. D.,
in the office of the Librarian of Congress at Washington.)

Although the entire universe has been arranged by the divine spirit for the expression of his purpose and all influences, in the end, work together for good, there are many imperfect manifestations of life that are difficult for the human mind to accept as being enacted under an absolutely just law.

Some human beings seem to be endowed with every blessing and possibility, as if the richest jewels in the heavenly casket had been selected for their especial benefit. Health, happiness and the realization of life's ambitions are as so many gifts of the gods scattered about them, while there are others who seemingly are deprived of nearly every blessing, conceived in iniquity, born in sin and reared under the most malign influences, the entire pathway of their life being strewn with misfortune, disappointment and disease.

The heights of the mountains and the depths of the valleys present no more striking contrasts than are everywhere seen in the demonstrations of human life. In fact, so apparent are these differences that the cursory observer will often declare that those who are blessed are basking in the smile of God, while those who are cursed by the weight of misfortune are resting under the ban of his wrath and disapproval; or, to borrow a theological phrase, some are the children of light, while others are the children of darkness. The world has never yet satisfactorily solved the problem of good and evil. The wisest philosopher of the past and the most profound of the present are as much at sea, upon this subject, as they were when they began its study.

And the reason for this is apparent. Men in trying to find God have studied the stars and all the external manifestations of the natural universe and, from what they have been able to observe, have formulated various theories, all of them more or less insufficient and incomplete. He who would find God must not seek him in the outer world, but look within, for there he will find the only manifestation of the divine that he will ever be able to recognize, and far more than, in the present state, he is able to comprehend or understand. So with any manifestation of divine law. To simply view the result without recognizing the cause is to reason from a wrong hypothesis, and to leave unrecognized the pivot upon which the whole matter turns.

We contend that there is no evil, in the absolute sense; that there are no mistakes and no accidents; everything that occurs is the result of some just cause, the outworking of which, in the end, cannot but result in good. Whatever expressions of life are seen upon this plane of existence are the best that can be made under the circumstances and, however futile they may appear, are but stepping stones to a still greater result that is destined to follow the attempt.

In the idiot we see what appears to be a failure. A life, in his case, given to the world apparently purposeless and valueless. He seems to be a breathing nonentity, unable to give or receive any pleasure or happiness. To him the world is an inconsequential one; the dull eyes, expressionless face and meaningless mutterings are of no interest to anyone, and yet, he has a spirit, has a destiny which he is fulfilling, as important, in the sum of things, as that of any other in the world.

An idiot child has as much intelligence as any other, the difference being that he is not able, through the physical environments in which his spirit is placed, to express either thoughts or intelligence. His spirit is connected to his body, but by such a narrow thread of life that each live without much relationship one with the other. The imperfect formation of the brain, which is due, usually, to some prenatal condition, shuts the door to all the aspirations of the spirit. In fact, the spirit is dumb, while the lips chatter on in a meaningless fashion. It is like a musical instrument, well enough constructed so far as shape and mechanism are concerned, but with only a note here and there that responds to the spirit.

To imagine that the spirit of the idiot does not understand what is passing on round about it, or hear what is said, is a mistake. It has the power to understand, but not the power to express. The treatment of those thus afflicted should be of the kindest and the gentlest character and, in many cases, where these laws are observed, the best results will follow.

An idiot, in short, is a child whose spirit is wholly out of relationship with the body save by a slight physical attraction which asserts itself with an inexorable force and, like an eagle chained to a rock, such a body holds the spirit. All that is harmonious will be helpful, all that is oppressive is bound to be injurious. Oftentimes, such a nature is responsive to some one or two attributes; music, flowers and children frequently exert an almost fascinating charm. Not much can be done except to conform to the laws of happiness and harmony as much as possible, realizing that the fault is not due to any curse of God, but to the ignorant violation of some law in nature.

We might say here, although it will convey but small meaning to the ordinary mind, that these partial incarnations are all significant, full of meaning and suggestive to the enlightened student of spiritual science; that in the various expressions the spirit makes at different times in the world's history, the complete and the incomplete, the satisfied and the unsatisfied, the high and the low, all furnish ultimately the foundation for the after success of the spirit.

PART VI.

INSANITY.

OBSESSION.

INSANITY.

(Entered according to Act of Congress, in the year 1893, by AUGUSTA W. FLETCHER, M. D., in the office of the Librarian of Congress at Washington.)

This is less understood than any other form of disease. We employ the word disease, since, although insufficient, it is more comprehensive than any other word that suggests itself.

In the insane person a complete change, both physical and spiritual, takes place, and is an illustration of an extreme discord that may exist between the spirit and the body. This discord arises from various causes; perhaps, from physical disease that so changes the entire chemicals of the body that there is little or no affiliation between it and the spirit, or, it may be, that great sorrow, accident, excitement or a variety of causes that are so positive in their character as to have wholly disturbed the spiritual relationship existing between the two great factors that constitute human life. Be assured that chemical changes have certainly taken place in the physical organization. The brain is no longer the same, the action of the heart and the circulation of the blood have undergone a change and, in a realm where there was once law and order, chaos and disruption now reign. The spirit has not the power to assert itself; the body has, strangely enough, gained the ascendency through the lack of spiritual influx it receives and, consequently, without attraction, moves on its way, carrying destruction and sorrow along with it. There will be times when, in the presence of some persons, the spirit will be able to very nearly assume its own control and the individual will, thereby, appear almost as sane as ever. He will live over old scenes, speak rationally and appear to have regained the seat of power; but remove him from the aforesaid presence, and the magnetic influence that it exerts, and the patient is worse than ever. The reason for this is plain. The magnetisms supplied by certain people are the very elements that the spirit wants, and while it is able to get them it regains its own naturalness of action and expression; for magnetism is but the essence of life, and contains all the elements that the spirit requires.

The present method of treating the insane is about the worst that could be suggested, for these persons are herded together in large institutions, sometimes hundreds under the same roof; the conditions that should be carefully observed are wholly ignored, and a sane person, subjected to the same association and rules for one year, would find it difficult to retain a hold over himself. The atmosphere is filled with the diseased elements that are thrown off and the body, without the positive action of the spirit, readily takes them on again. The reason why so few persons are discharged as cured from these institutions, is due to this cause.

There should be a great similarity between the treatment of the insane and that of the criminal. Every jail becomes a school of crime through a lack of proper classification of the criminals and because the entire influence generated is of the criminal order. This state of things exists to a greater degree in the hospitals of the insane, where those who are only partially affected are placed with others who are hopelessly so, and thus two organizations, that should be as widely separated as the poles, are brought into close juxtaposition with each other.

A large percentage of the mild form of insanity could be remedied and, in many cases, absolutely cured if the patient could be removed from discordant surroundings and placed under harmonious circumstances. Whatever medical science can do to regulate the body should be done, but in effecting a cure, the spirit must be directly appealed to. Everything that will call it into active relationship with the body should be done and as little restraint placed over the patient as possible. Hard-hearted and cruel keepers and unsympathetic attendants should be persons unknown in these reformatories. In fact, if we are to have these institutions at all, let them be managed and conducted by those whose perceptions are developed, and whose general temperament is helpful and kind.

Some of the blackest horrors that mark this most progressive civilization are the result of investigations into the conduct of these asylums. Positions are held, not according to the fitness of the individual, but through his social and political influence, and gross neglect, utter ignorance and absolute barbarity stand forth, in all their horrors, when the kindly hand lifts the curtain that shields these institutions from the public gaze.

Persons acting in the capacity of attendants in such places should be properly educated and trained for their work, and at the first exhibition of cruelty should be disqualified for that position. The more sunshine, the more harmony, the more peaceful associations that you can surround the patient with, the quicker you can induce a harmonious relationship between his spirit and his body.

What we have said thus far, relates to persons mildly affected, and now we shall deal with the extreme cases, furnishing an explanation which will, in part, apply to all to a degree, and this explanation, we are aware, will be discountenanced by all those who have not, as yet, entered into an acceptation of the spirit being the governing law. And this brings us to the consideration of

Obsession.

(Entered according to Act of Congress, in the year 1893, by AUGUSTA W. FLETCHER, M. D., in the office of the Librarian of Congress at Washington.)

By obsession we mean the possession of the human body—the full and the partial possession of the human body—by some spirit foreign in its nature and character to the rightful spiritual possessor thereof. In order for this to be understood, it must be recognized as a fact that death is a physical and not a spiritual condition and that, consequently, every spirit that has existed on the earth plane still moves in the atmosphere of the earth, although the body which it inhabited may long since have crumbled to dust. Such spirits manifest the same desires, proclivities, attractions and repulsions after death as before and, since the earth and its conditions furnish an agreeable plane of action, they are all the time endeavoring to establish relationship with a body more or less like the one which they inhabited when here.

Instead of the spiritual world being filled with angels and archangels, who pass their time in waving palms and chanting praises, it is, in fact, a reproduction of this world; or, to speak exactly, we should say that the earth is a reflection of the spirit-spheres that surround the earth. There are high spirits and low spirits, good and bad. The higher the spirit the more removed from the earth and earthly gratifications; the lower the spirit the closer associated with the earth. High spirits return with the purpose of serving humanity, while low spirits return with the idea of gratifying themselves. As the earth is continually sending numberless spirits of this latter order to the spirit world, it is not strange that they should attempt to return to the sphere of their earthly enjoyments again.

"Are they not restrained by the law of God?" asks one. They are not restrained from doing evil on that plane of life, any more than they are on this. God sustains the same relationship to all spheres of life, and each spirit is allowed to work out his desire until the intelligence is developed to that degree wherein, from choice, he ceases to do evil because he loves to do well. Happiness, then, not becoming a gift dependent upon the goodness of God, but a just inheritance bestowed upon individual work and endeavor.

But to return, these undeveloped spirits, while in close association with the earth, reaffiliate themselves with every circumstance and individual wherein exists the smallest physical attraction for them. Over every jail, over every prison, around every corner grogshop and den of infamy they congregate, seeking to find some organization with which they can associate themselves and, thereby, gratify their old earthly desires. If they find an organization out of harmony with itself, which furnishes any attraction for them whatever, they immediately assume control of it, disconnecting the spirit that belongs therein and assuming the reins of control themselves. Consequently, the patient manifests attributes wholly inconsistent with what you formerly knew of him. He hates his best friends and loves the things which, in other days, he used to abhor. In fact, the physical countenance will become so changed that you will scarcely be able to recognize it. In dealing, then, with this matter, you have a third element which is not recognized by the medical science of the present day; for, to them, the cause of disease exists within the individual, and is dealt with alone from that standpoint. It has only been recently that psychical influences have been recognized as producing a strong effect upon the nervous system of highly sensitive people, and when this idea was first suggested, it was as much derided as, no doubt, our present proposition will be, which is, that in severe cases of insanity the spirit is wholly thrown out of connection with the body, and another spirit, for which that body furnishes some attraction, but with an influence more or less foreign to it, steps in and takes its place, manifesting all the idiosyncrasies, hates, likes and peculiarities of a distinctive mind. In fact, this new controlling spirit fails to recognize either duties, persons or surroundings, but has brought, with itself, its own past, which, with difficulty, it is trying to fit down to the present.

One of the peculiarities of insane people is, that while in excited states, they seem bent upon self-destruction. This is looked upon as a natural symptom and neither the friends nor the physicians are surprised at it; but there is a far deeper cause than mere mental peculiarity. This foreign spirit finds itself in a sphere which, after it has occupied it for a time, becomes distasteful. It cannot get away from the attraction that was exerted over it in the first instance, and these determined efforts at self-destruction are the spirit's attempts to free itself from its undesirable environments. With great cunning it seeks to further this end, for, having lived independent of the body, it brings back to physical life a keener perception and deeper penetration than is possessed by most persons and, consequently, unless a very stringent guard is kept over the patient, he will, sooner or later, accomplish his purpose. And thus the spirit will again find the freedom it craves.

There are other forms of insanity where the patient is continually manifesting different individualities. One day he is a musician; the next a soldier and the next some one else, and so on *ad infinitum*. These different proclivities, so called, reappear at given intervals and take up the thread where it has been broken off. Such individuals are the playthings of a number of undeveloped spirits, who only leave to make place for others. The departing spirits never get wholly out of the atmosphere of the person thus afflicted, but are in constant association with him.

Some one will ask, where is the original spirit to whom this physical body belonged in the first place? As much removed from it as though separated by death, is our answer; for life is simply the attraction of these two opposite conditions. Were it possible to bring about the same physical condition as existed when both spirit and body were harmoniously united, the spirit would, without doubt, be attracted back to its old centre of action and, as we have before said, the only conditions that are likely to bring about this result are dependent upon the establishment of complete magnetic attractions. This is one of the most difficult achievements known, and there are few instances in which it has ever been carried out with success. Kindness, sympathetic care and plenty of outdoor life are the only suggestions that we can offer in a general way.

When human beings are taught that the other world is what they make it, and that a life upon earth is but the laying of the foundation of what is to follow, instead of its being impressed upon their minds that the church has the power of conferring absolution, life will be more practically serious here and, consequently, supply the requisite elements for greater happiness in the hereafter.

PART VII.

THE MYSTERY OF SLEEP.

DO WE TRAVEL WHEN WE SLEEP?

THE MYSTERY OF SLEEP.

(Entered according to Act of Congress, in the year 1893, by AUGUSTA W. FLETCHER, M. D.,
in the office of the Librarian of Congress at Washington.)

'Tis beautiful to leave the world awhile
　For the soft visions of the gentle night;
And free, at last, from mortal care or guile,
　To live as only in the angels' sight,
In sleep's sweet realm so costly shut in,
Where, at the worst, we only *dream* of sin !—SAXE.

Sleep is nature's sweet restorer; but how it restores, and what the process is, may interest those who constantly observe its action, yet never give its occurrence more than a passing thought.

The body is one thing and the spirit another. The body, without the action of the spirit, would be no more intelligent than are the myriads of other forms of physical life that move and breathe over the face of the earth. It has no particular destiny of its own and, without the actuating power of the spirit, would prove of no more interest than a tree, a flower or any other chemical association of elements that are held together only to serve a purpose beyond themselves, and whose character the wise are not in the least able to comprehend.

The real man is the spiritual man, the real self, the spiritual self. The *ego* and the spirit are synonymous, and the body, important as it is, only becomes of importance when it ministers to and is directed by the spirit itself.

The spirit can exist and perform its work without the body; in fact, intelligent physical life is only one phase of the spiritual life. Without the spirit the body cannot sustain any relationship with physical life. By partially withdrawing the spirit, weakness and disease are the result; wholly withdraw it and death follows. That, in turn, is succeeded by complete disintegration of all the physical elements. It must be kept continually in mind that the body is the negative factor, the spirit the positive, in this scheme of human life, and the work that is done is accomplished, primarily, by the spirit, the body being only the instrument used to assist in its fulfillment. It is the spirit that trains the hand until it fully obeys its mandates and responds at once to its inspiration. The hand of the artist differs not from the hand of any other man, but the spirit of the artist is of far different quality. That spirit within has clothed itself with matter and immediately begins to reveal itself, through the medium of the flesh, upon this external plane of existence. The spirit within perceives the beauty and grandeur of the life without, and at once begins to educate the hand to reproduce it.

Standing before the silent canvas, the warmth and glow and spirit of the Summer are gradually wrought out, until the beauty of nature stands reflected. There is something more than the mere arrangement of color in the creation. The artist must absolutely feel what he is doing and into it put a part of himself. And thus around the works of all true artists there is a something which can never be described and which no copyist, however exact, can ever quite reproduce. It is a stamp of his own spiritual individuality which the cunning of his hand has transferred to the canvas and, thereby, disconnected from himself.

This law runs through the entire scheme of existence; spirit acting, matter acted upon. In the phenomenon of life these two are united, in sleep they are partially separated and in death wholly so. The spirit, in the early part of the day, is full of magnetic force derived from higher realms, from the atmosphere and surrounding earthly conditions and, full of enthusiasm, begins its work. It is more positive at that time and is, accordingly, fresher in its activities. Gradually, this diminishes until, at night, the spirit (not the body) has exhausted its force and strength. The atmosphere no longer presents elements that the spirit can assimilate with itself. The magnetism that the body generates has been exhausted and it is forced to retire within itself. Consequently, it removes the body from the distraction of the surroundings of the day and, in a reclining position, gradually withdraws itself from its seat of power in order, through this partial disassociation, to gather up from various sources the elements required for work on the coming morrow. In what is called health this is readily accomplished and the body is thrown into a hypnotic state by its own spirit and left to rest. The spirit withdraws into one or more of the spiritual states that it is responsive to, and lives the truest and the highest part of its existence without the impediment and incumbrance of the body itself. Do not understand us to mean that the spirit is wholly disassociated from the body, for, if that was the case, death would immediately ensue. It is, at such times, only partially disconnected, so that, in unusual physical disturbances which would disarrange the magnetic waves that surround the body, it would call the spirit back to its seat of power. But all influences being equal, and the surroundings harmonious and quiet, the spirit is able to carry out its own will and purposes, visit countries far distant, meet and associate with individuals never known in waking moments and, oftentimes, foreshadow events which the future serves to fulfill.

Dream life is the ideal life, wherein the spirit rises far above the petty contentions of the day and time, bursts all bonds of limitation, and is swung far out upon that immeasurable sea on whose waves so many possibilities float which never find realization in the world of things. But sleep does not always come at will, nor when the apparent necessary conditions are made for it. The condition of the body and the incomplete relationship of the spirit thereto, sometimes prevents the disassociation of one from the other, or makes that disconnection so imperfect as to render continuous slumber an impossibility. In such cases, every effort should be put forth to make the hours before retiring as harmonious and peaceful as possible. If it is not within one's self to be at peace with the annoyances of the day, which, like so many restless ghosts, will not be laid, then the introduction of some other influence becomes a necessity. The individual can do very much for himself in this particular direction. He can make his will positive to all unpleasant thoughts, by turning his mind toward happier and sweeter ones, and thus the old idea, too fast falling into disuse, of singing an evening hymn or offering a soulful prayer before retiring, furnishes a fit preparation for the harmonious slumbers that should follow.

The magnetic healer is able to bring the body into harmonious relationship with the indwelling spirit and, thereby, enable the spirit to withdraw itself as it desires. The sleep induced by this same magnetic influence is the most restful and pleasurable known. Narcotics and drugs are fast giving way to it and, in time, they will be wholly discontinued. The effect which their use induces is but temporary and, in the end, far from beneficial.

If, for any reason, sleep is not, or cannot be, induced it is only a question of a short time when a disarrangement of the entire human machine will follow; there being so much friction between the spirit and the body, that all the reserved force is used up, and it begins to show signs of wearing out. Sleep is really a lubricant for the physical machinery. If no oil is put on the various parts of an engine, or any other machine, it becomes only a question of a short time as to what the result will be. Great nervous irritability, mental derangement and insanity are some of the numerous evils that follow in the train of a perversion of the law of nature. The force of the spirit must be withdrawn from the body from six to ten hours, at least, out of the twenty-four, and we make this statement unconditionally, for we see the importance of its observance.

The body, during the hours of slumber, is not infrequently played upon by the myriads of invisible influences which pervade the atmosphere appertaining to the earth, and which the partial disassociation of the individual spirit bestows an added power upon. Such spirits have great power over some individuals, and commit serious offences against the welfare and health of the body, impairing it, sometimes, to such a degree as to induce severe illness and distress. The *somnambule* is an illustration of this law. A spirit, who is more or less in affinity with the body, watches for its opportunity and, when the spirit which rightly belongs there is sufficiently removed, it gradually insinuates itself until it gains a positive control of it; the spirit which rightfully belongs to the body has almost no power to assert itself over it, consequently, this invader starts out, unchecked, upon its expedition of personal gratification. It takes the body to unknown heights, or precipitates it into destruction, always achieving some result which would be utterly impossible in waking moments. Generally, these influences are of a low and designing order, as their actions would plainly evidence. There are, however, some exceptions to the rule, and we have known persons who have been influenced while in sleep and used for the perfection of artistic and literary work which was wholly beyond their working capacity.

Do We Travel When We Sleep?

(Entered according to Act of Congress, in the year 1893, by AUGUSTA W. FLETCHER, M. D.,
in the office of the Librarian of Congress at Washington.)

Assuredly, and that is where the renewed strength, the fresh impressions and new-born determinations are found. Your spirit, when freed from its physical environments, is able to go where it pleases, to see what it pleases and, oftentimes, to bring back into waking moments the result of these experiences as a spirit. You may, while the body sleeps, cross the ocean, wander through distant lands, look upon scenes, think thoughts, accomplish results and forecast future endeavors, without having the slightest relationship exist between them and your waking moments. Ten years afterward you may, *in propria personæ*, step on board an ocean steamer, cross the seas and visit these same scenes, realizing, all the time that you are there, a certain sense of familiarity, feeling that you know the places, have a fancied recognition, even, of some of the people, and for all this you can offer no clear explanation. Your spirit is simply recalling what it has seen before and mirroring it upon your external consciousness.

The inventor is, perhaps, the most practical dreamer of all, for the best inventions of the present day, those which have done more to revolutionize the entire system of labor and trade, have been found in dream-life. The electric light, whose brilliancy is only equaled by the stars in the heavens, and the wonderful telephone, that transmits a whisper from one State to another, were only the dreams of an enthusiast, until they were actualized down to the necessities of the age.

The truth is, all the higher minds on earth move in a spiritual sphere commensurate with their ambitions and desires. Awake, they catch only the reflection of those spheres; asleep, they dwell within their limits. Every picture that is painted, every house that is built and every invention that is made, has its existence, spiritually, before it lives in the outer world of reality. Awake, the inventor finds himself reaching out for the something that is lacking; asleep, he is in the realm of that something and is able to fit it in its respective place.

Dreams, then, in the first instance, are the experiences of the spirit itself; but you will say they are not always of the high order that you have referred to, for they present all the varying lights and shadows of the lowest, as well as the highest, conditions of human life, unknown to your waking moments, but induced and experienced in sleep. This is, without doubt, true; but for it there is ample explanation. The spirit is seeing all the phases of life within, above and below its present form, and the horrors that are realized with so much vividness that the impression lasts for months are actual scenes through which the spirit passes in its journey through the spiritual universe.

If you stop, for one moment, to consider the varying conditions of physical life around you, you will readily realize that, if there be a spiritual counterpart for all of this, the spirit in visiting and viewing them will perceive as great a contrast, if not greater, than you see from the earthly standpoint. Thoughts and desires are the realities of the spiritual world. The spirit can send a thought, freighted with either good or ill, more readily than you can pass a book from one hand to the other. The air is full of the thoughts of men, and those who are sensitive are bound to catch the impressions as they pass through it. In the city, where there are hurrying crowds of men, the atmosphere is bound to be full of their selfish and mercenary thoughts. The church is bound to exert a heavy, sombre influence which will be depressing to all, save those whose sublime egotism lead them to use it as a stepping stone to future greatness. Around every cesspool of vice where crime and sin drag themselves through the unholy hours of the night, and where selfishness and lustful desires rule with unquestioned sway, there are invisible influences of the most diabolical and depressing character. The drunkard, in the last throes of delirium tremens, is giving you no imaginary picture when he turns, in horror, from the vipers and reptiles that seemingly assail him. Through the excessive gratification of his desire for drink he has reduced himself to the plane where these forms of life exist, and they are spiritual verities to him. What wonder, then, when the spirit starts out in its nightly journey through space, that it, in passing through these different gradations of spiritual life, encounters all the horrors that therein abound, plays a strange part and returns, in the waking moments, weary and depleted. How many times have you not said, "I feel completely worn out to-day; I had a fearful dream last night?"

Just the same as in visiting the crime-stricken portions of your city, you return home, feeling it is almost impossible to enjoy the luxuries you find there, because of the miseries you have just seen.

Whatever has been is. The spiritual world is a mighty book of remembrance, upon whose pages every passing event is depicted with marvelous accuracy and care. The past and present are as one, and the battles and the victories of the other ages live as if they only occurred to-day. Thus the spirit, in entering the spiritual world, is able to view these different scenes. On waking, the individual is not able to realize the connection, nor yet comprehend the import; but what is called imagination, which, in reality, has no existence, is simply the reflection of some spiritual state which the sensitive brain gets but an imperfect view of. All that is seen in dreams has existed or is existing at the present time.

More care should be taken of the body during sleep than at any other time in the twenty-four hours. Place the head of the bed toward the east, in a room as far removed from external influences and confusion as possible. Bear in mind to pass an hour or two, before retiring, under quiet and reassuring influences. Disconnect yourself from every scene or contending thought, put your mind *en rapport* with some place. theme or person that may have pleasurable and endearing associations for you, and float out upon the sea of invisible and conscious life, gathering therefrom spiritual strength with which to meet the duties of the morrow.

PART VIII.

WHAT IS DEATH?

WHAT IS DEATH?
IS IT A DESTROYER OR A BUILDER?

<small>(Entered according to Act of Congress, in the year 1898, by AUGUSTA W. FLETCHER, M. D., in the office of the Librarian of Congress at Washington.)</small>

There are two mighty currents that sweep over the ocean of life, one ebbing, the other flowing. One bears upon its bosom a little bark, full of promise, full of things to be, of hopes, joys, victories and defeats; the other bears away a life whose drama has been finished, be it long or short, with all the expressed and the unexpressed about it. And he who stands looking on asks, of the former, whence, and of the latter, whither. Life and death, activity and inertia, day and night, things begun and things ended, tears and joy for one, tears and sorrow for the other.

Of life, little is known beyond its expression here on the earth plane. It seems to be its own arbiter, to a great degree, evolves its own law and inexorably closes the volume in defiance of every earthly protest or desire. Philosophers deal with it only from its earthly side, drawing conclusions from causes that the wisest but dimly understand. Theologians find in these two great events a wide field for speculative thought, which, during the past centuries, they have not failed to improve. They have devised a system of creation, rewards and punishments to be continued beyond the grave, which, although in defiance of both reason and common sense, has exerted a strange and inexplicable influence over the human mind. The world at large has an undefined sense that birth is not the beginning nor death the end; but this is rather the result of a desire for a continuance of life, than a law subject to demonstration.

The fear of death is due to the lack of knowledge as to what it really is. The sense of some awful doom which eternity holds, like the sword of Damocles, suspended over the head of each offender and which, on the day of judgment, will fall, producing never-ending pain, makes the strong man tremble, in fear and terror, on the portals of that great mystery through which the piercing eye of science has not been able to penetrate. The worst penalty that can be inflicted by governments against those who break important laws is death, even while the same judge who pronounces the death sentence, reads from the bible, "Thou shalt not kill." Could some hand but raise the curtain that separates the known from the unknown, the earthly from the spiritual, and bring man face to face with that which follows death, he would render unto this age, and all subsequent ages, such a boon as has never before been vouchsafed to the world. Could some voice, from beyond the veil, break the long eternities of silence and project a message of courage and hope to those who, with faltering steps, are following after him, his name would sound in songs of praise for all time. And yet, the purpose of life, or, at least, one of the purposes, is to solve the mystery that everywhere surrounds it. To lay aside superstition and ignorance, which, oftentimes, forms the major part of man's life, and study this subject quietly and dispassionately, following wherever the highest conclusions will lead, whether to the foot of the altar, upon which every form of sacrifice has been made, or into the field of blank materialism, where hope and aspiration sink, like so many stars, never to rise again.

Let us consider the subject from the standpoint of nature. In so-called inanimate life, the same law applies as to life in its more advanced stages. The flowers, trees and animals possess an internal impulse which is as faithful to the fulfilling of the purpose as is the spirit of man to the outworking of its destiny. These forms of life, classified, as they are, by a superior intelligence, presumably select their own conditions, attract and assimilate the elements they require from the soil and the atmosphere, and go on their way outworking a result which never varies from the original intention. In the course of time we die; that is to say, the magnet of life, whatever it may be, no longer attracts elements to itself, and at the point where this attraction ceases disorganization and disintegration begin. But following out the action of these two laws, so similar in their character, you will not find that they are destroying a single element; but, instead, are preparing the old elements to take on another form of expression, which shall be, to them, a round higher in the ladder of life.

Death, then, has taken nothing from the laboratory of nature; it simply takes up the elements that life has left, and arranges for another form of life. Thus her resources are never exhausted. The equipoise is always maintained, the supply is equal to the demand, and nothing is either lost or gained in the world of material, during all the cycles of time. The wisest man in the world has not the power of destroying a single element, but may change its form and displace the arrangement; for what is is, has been and always will be.

I hold in my hand a piece of wood; the elements constituting the wood are held in bondage and have not the power of acting independently of each other. I cast the bit of wood into the flame and watch it being slowly consumed thereby. When this process is completed, have I destroyed the wood? As a piece of wood, yes; but the elements that constituted it, and were enslaved, are set free by the action of combustion, and they start out on a higher career than that which marked their former existence. Destroyed? No. Changed, uplifted, set free? Yes. From this example, it will be seen that, through the law of evolution, death becomes a stepping-stone of life, and that throughout all the physical universe these great processes have enabled this and all other planets to arrive at their present state of development, and will be the power whereby still mightier results shall be obtained. The ordinary mind will not grasp easily, or accept readily, the law of evolution. Darwin, Huxley, Tyndall, and Spencer are all personalities which the unthinking fear; whose hands have, with the wand of truth, during the present century, destroyed so many idols and temples. These men, great and wise as they are, and in whose praise too much cannot be said, have only taken one side of the subject. They have reasoned logically as far as they have gone, but have not completed the journey. They have all led up to human life; they have begun from the lowest point, have journeyed far and wide, until they reached man, and then stopped. That science that can read the story of the stars, the history of the planet upon which you stand, analyze the drop of water, aye, the very air you breathe, stands before the open grave with closed eyes and sealed lips, without the ability to take one single step over its threshold into the future. But science, in the age that is to come, must cross this threshold and penetrate into the depths of the life beyond, so that the spiritual world shall be as logically understood as are the more material planets that make up the system.

Mankind, to-day, is looking toward science to solve the problem which, in earlier days, was relegated to ecclesiastical judges. Even the church, after preaching immortality for centuries and assuming that man never dies, is endeavoring to find proof of its assertion entirely outside its own province. Science can, when it recognizes the spiritual side of life, easily accomplish this great purpose for the world, by remembering that the spirit is first, that matter is only a means of its expression, that this planet, this material world, is but the instrument in the hands of the spiritual world; that every blade of grass, every singing bird, and every human being, is but an expression of the same forces, differing in degree of enfoldment, but, through the action of the law of evolution, forever creeping along the pathway of progress to the ultimate, which is but the turning-point of a newer and greater destiny. In man, we find the realization of matter and spirit.

Without spirit, matter is expressionless and void; with spirit, it takes its place among the mighty realities of the world, guiding, shaping and influencing the destiny of all things and all persons that are responsive to it.

During the younger years of life, the spirit is gaining possession of its machine; during the latter years, they work in harmony with each other, and the best work of life is accomplished between the years of twenty-five and fifty. In that time, in most cases, the spirit has become responsive to higher attractions than the earth offers, and the subsequent years, be they few or many, are passed in the effort of the spirit to gradually relieve itself from physical environments, so as to take on the higher spiritual ones, for which the experiences of life have finally fitted it, and when death comes it is simply the completion of a process which has been going on for a long time.

Sudden illnesses, as they are called, are mistaken interpretations of physical conditions. What appears to be sudden illness is the result of a condition through which the body has been passing and, at a given point, the elements of disease reveal themselves, although they were lurking in the system all the time. The healthy man is one whose body is entirely under the magnetic control of his spirit. If this control can always be sustained he will remain so until the end. Wherever the spirit loses its hold over physical elements, there the power of disease or disintegration begins. If the spirit be conscious of this in time, it will be able to assume its old control and expel the offender; but if not, then the power creeps on, gains the ascendency, and death ensues. Which means that the spirit no longer inhabits the tenement of clay, for the old relationship and connections have ceased to exist, and that the body, like the billet of wood, has been tossed into the flame, in order to free the elements which are therein contained, and give them an opportunity to take on new forms of life; while the spirit, freed from earthly conditions, by a law of spiritual gravitation, at once enters in upon that state which its development entitles it to.

Yesterday, my friend was alive and well; we journeyed together in pleasant converse, and he seemed to be in accord with all the surroundings. To-day, I stand beside him, I take his hand in mine, I speak to him, I call him by old-time names, and conjure up many pleasant memories of happy days gone by. But he answers me not; the eyes are closed and the lips are sealed; he is the same and not the same. And wherein is the difference? Yesterday, it was the body of my friend acted upon by the spirit that dwelt within; to-day, the lifeless thing before me is the body of the same man, but that which made it dear and gave it intelligence has passed out of relationship and, in a higher sphere, has taken upon itself new duties, new obligations and new purposes.

Have you ever watched the process of a spirit passing from this world to the world of light? Have you ever seen, as the sands of the hour-glass run low, the transmission of life from the earthly to the spiritual plane? The dying man lies upon a bed of illness; already the glassy eyes, the worn features and the heavy breath betray the presence of that great change through whose power of disintegration all earthly beings are leveled. Anxious friends and loving hearts look on with tender sympathy, witnessing the action of a law which they are unable to understand. Just above the heart of the sufferer a faint light is seen. Gradually it extends upward toward the head, and downward toward the feet, connected to the physical body by numerous lines of light. As the patient grows weaker this object becomes more distinct. Soon the individuality is more in the spiritual than the material world, and the human lips will murmur of those who lived in the past and were loved by him, declaring that they are present and that they have come to take him away. And so the sands of life flow on and, at last, the weary eyes are closed with the slumber that knows no waking, and the indwelling spirit has left its earthly habitation and passed into that more ethereal body which has been building itself through all the years of life. And then this spirit will pass on through the various phases of spiritual development, with which this article has nothing to do beyond indicating, but which, to the spiritual student, whose eyes are strong enough to view it, is revealed a grandeur of which the earthly mind has never yet received an intimation.

Death is the stepping-stone to the higher life, is the dropping of a physical covering to take on a more refined one, is the leaving of the narrow limitations of earth for the wider fields of action in other realms, is the loss of nothing that is good, is the ability to ever conquer and overcome that which is bad, is an open door through which the spirit passes, with hurrying steps, to find the treasures earth had not the power to keep, is a land in which a just realization of all things can be seen, where motives stand superior to results, and where the ideal becomes, in time, the real.

After death there is no punishment but that which comes as the inevitable result of life's laws perverted. Wrongs done and evils enacted are followed by consequences as inevitable as is the mantle of God's glory that falls around each life that has devoted its endeavors to noble living. But, however dark the sphere in which the spirit finds itself, the beckoning hand of angels will gradually call it from darkness into the light.

There are two objects in life which have more to do with moulding the future destiny of man than would seem, at first, to be apparent. One, consists in developing the resources of the external life, to which all the energies are bent and the higher ambition sacrificed, the other, relates to the development of the interior spiritual man, the building up of the temple within, and the unfolding of the aspirations of the spirit. The latter, in fact, being the only real life, before which the transitory things of earth fade like the mist before the glory of the rising sun. These two traits, as they might be called, are really opposed to each other; they rarely walk hand in hand together, and where one is, the other is not. The first relates wholly to this world; the second to this world, it is true, but has its continuation in all worlds and higher forms of life.

You see men every day working, striving and crucifying the higher self, for the purpose of building up a certain temporary, material power and fearing the hand of poverty, knowing the strength that wealth gives; no task is too severe for them to undertake to place them well before their fellows. Thus, with this object in view, life becomes, with the one, a constant endeavor to accumulate money and, during all the years that follow, this thought is held to with wonderful tenacity. Love, sympathy and every sweet association and, in fact, the entire sentimental side of life, are looked upon as the pretty things which the practical mind has no time to indulge in. They are too expensive, not that they cost much, but they take up time that might, otherwise, be devoted to different purposes. And so the nature becomes hard, stolid, unsympathetic and embittered, until, in fact, when the object of life is, to a great measure, realized, the power to enjoy it has become weakened, if not altogether lost. If you look out into the busy street in the morning you will see crowds of men hurrying along, apparently indifferent to each other, their faces hard and set, their eyes dulled to every influence that may be pleasing or beautiful around them, and the whole strength of their being concentrated upon the accomplishment of some purely material result. They jostle each other in the market-places, they tear each other down that they may build themselves up and their days become one long, weary struggle to outrun their fellows in the race for wealth. Ask any of these, "For what are you working?" and he will reply, "Oh, I am working to accomplish a result, and when that is done I shall be happy." But no sooner is the amount accumulated, which in the beginning seemed to contain the realization of all his dreams, than a still greater sum suggests itself. In fact, the happiness of the miser can be said to lie in the next bag of gold which he has not obtained, and the next and so on, it always being just beyond his reach.

Death comes to such a man, as it does to every other, in time, and he enters into the spiritual world. The only thing he was possessed of belonged to the material world. Concerning the passage of such an one into the other life, the commentator wrote wisely, when he said, "he has left all he had," since the currency of eternity is neither gold nor silver. This spirit who may have been, when on earth, high in office and respected of men, finds himself gravitating to the point where he absolutely belongs and, having no spiritual attainments, he is still in the thought of the great object of his life.

We have in mind a man, like unto the above, who came to the spiritual world having lived an earthly career full of prosperity and success. Gold had been his God; he had struggled for it by day and dreamed of it at night; it was, in fact, all he knew, and all he wished or cared for. His one regret, on leaving the earth, was that he must drop a great financial scheme out of which millions might have been made. But all the wealth of the Indies, the wisdom of medical science, and the prayers said for him, were not able to buy a single moment of time. He awoke to find himself in a large cave lined throughout with gold; under his feet, over his head, wherever he turned, he saw himself reflected in the shining metal, that to him had always been so valuable. It was gold, hard and unyielding.

Through an opening in the side he could see the sun shining and hear the distant murmur of happy voices. Formerly this had meant nothing to him, but now they sounded very pleasant to his ear. Looking again, he beheld the faces dear to him in earlier days; father, mother, wife and children, all in sweet accord, whispering his name and calling him to them. He turned to go, but as he sought to take the first step a bar of gold blocked the way and an angel stood beside him saying, "thou must conquer the ambitions of earth before thou canst realize the joys of heaven. When thou hast grown to see that material things are only valuable when they serve a spiritual purpose, then shalt thou find greater joy in love and peace than all the wealth that the world can give." And so he struggled on until human selfishness was conquered, and the spirit of greed eliminated.

Another man living in the world, moving in the same surroundings, and breathing the same air, might be able to see the hollowness of all earthly things, and value a good character above great wealth. Honor, truth, love and justice will then be more than words to him, and he will place that high value upon himself that, instead of fearing, by any act, that he will lose the respect of the world, he will strive for something infinitely greater, his own self-respect. Such an one will give courage to the faint-hearted, will strengthen the weak, comfort the sorrowing and, in passing into the other world, will be able to carry with him the results of a life well lived, which will be to his soul what wings are to the bird, ever lifting it into the clearer air and a broader view.

A wise man, holding a child by the hand, is walking through the town. The child looks toward a great mansion where a rich man lives.

"Whose house is that, father?" asks the boy.

"It is the house of a rich man, and a man who, rising from a condition of the direst poverty, has made himself feared by those less fortunate."

The child pointed to another building where the poor are fed and the sick cared for, asking again:

"Whose house is that?"

"That is a house, my child, that a good man built by the help of every good man, as a place of refuge for the unfortunate and suffering children of earth."

"Can every one be rich?" repeated the child, inquiringly.

"No," replied the wise man, thoughtfully. "No, every man cannot be great and rich and powerful, but every man can be good and true if he wishes."

"And which is it better to be?" repeated the child.

"The world will some day ask that question most seriously. Greatness born of things lives, dies and is forgotten in the world of things; but goodness is the invisible witness, heaven-sent, which speaks to the heart of man and lives throughout eternity at oneness with God himself," answered the old man.

And so they moved on their appointed way, but the great truth spoken has echoed through the world ever since.

Thus it will be seen that the life is more than the raiment; that the hereafter depends upon the HERE, and that death, instead of being the end of anything, is but the continuance of all things. The purpose of the church has been to prepare man for death; works counted for little, faith in the creed for much. "Repent, for to-morrow ye die," has been sounded through the past centuries by every ecclesiastical teacher extant. Repent of evil, since repentance is both wise and good, not because death comes to-morrow, but rather because the spirit yearns to break away from the shackles of wrong-doing and wrong-thinking, wherever they may be.

We hold that no man is fit to die until he has really learned how to live, for when death comes it is to take you from the Winter land to the Summer land. It comes not to destroy that which is, but to construct and build something grander than that which has been, to help you to see the mistakes of life and bring the desire to conquer and overcome them, to show you how, through its devious ways, the guiding power of wisdom was directing your footsteps and revealing the purpose of every dark and sad experience, which, like so many stepping-stones, have served to carry you forward, to reveal to you the never-ending eternity that stretches onward from one height to another, and allures you by the charm of a greater nobility and power. Death is not the enemy of man, it is his best friend. Death is the kindly frost that cracks the shell and leaves the kernel room to germinate.

PART IX.

MODERN SPIRITUALISM.

MODERN SPIRITUALISM.

(Entered according to Act of Congress, in the year 1893, by AUGUSTA W. FLETCHER, M. D.,
in the office of the Librarian of Congress at Washington.)

This is a subject which we approach with considerable diffidence, since it has been so imperfectly understood and subjected to the foolish criticisms of those who comprehend, not at all, its far-reaching and comprehensive philosophy. That there have been many devotees of spiritualism who have held extraordinary ideas, and who have been most persistent in announcing them, is true, and that there has been but an imperfect statement of its real principles is likewise a fact. But this is due to various causes, which any intelligent mind will readily see and admit. However, this should have nothing whatever to do with the justness of its claims impartially and consistently stated. That individuals have erred from the path of right—gone wrong, as the world says—does not at all affect the validity of the claim, that modern spiritualism is the religion of all religions with something added to it. Without entering into the vast array of objections and arguments which have grown up on every hand, we shall state, in as few words as possible, what spiritualism is.

The universe is an expression of the divine mind, and the best that could be made under the existing conditions. Every human being is an emanation of the divine, outworking its purpose in the spaces above and below the earth, and all the powers of life within the earth are pervaded by the unseen influence of this divine presence. There is, consequently, no division of supremacy, no power of evil; but each human being is possessed of the lesser good to be overcome by the greater.

Every soul is an entity in itself, responsive to the centre of life. Life itself, in the eternal, being but a series of experiences through which the soul passes, in its connection with matter, for the rounding out and the completion of the spirit, which is the soul's expression through matter. What appear to be lower forms of life in the human, are really newer forms of life; that is to say, the advanced spirit differs only from the unadvanced, inasmuch as, in the first case, the possibilities have been developed through earthly experiences and, in the second, are awaiting such development. The more that man accomplishes in any one physical existence, the further he is removed from the necessity of physical life; but he must grow spiritual within himself, and can never receive any direct outside help, save that which will show him how he can, by his own individual efforts, attain the desired end, which is the overcoming of self, the unfolding of the individual, and the upbuilding of that moral structure which enables the intelligent man to penetrate, by the clear eye of the spirit, the dross of external life and perceive the work which underlies it and which, ultimately, will result in universal good.

In place, then, of vicarious atonement, either in this world or the next, man is thrown upon his own individual responsibility, and is made to feel that whatever salvation he gets, either in this or other worlds, is dependent upon his daily life.

"What shall I do to be saved?" cries the frightened sinner.

"Believe in Jesus and our creed," replies the church.

"What shall I do to be saved?" asks the intelligent man.

"Do as near right as you can, and salvation is yours," replies spiritualism.

In fact, it is the reversal of the whole scheme. The church insists upon faith, and spiritualism insists upon life and right living, holding that any man who has done his best to live uprightly has redeemed himself from sin every time that he has resisted sin; and that when he has allowed himself to depart from the paths of right, he has simply placed a barrier between himself and the happiness that right doing is bound to bring. All this relates as much to the present as to the future, for the religion that does not deal with man's present need surely presents a doubtful possibility of satisfying his future necessity.

The material universe exists quite as much as a part of the divine plan as does the spiritual, and instead of modern science being the enemy of true religion it is its firmest and best friend. He who discovers a law in nature, and gives it to the world, can justly be called a divinely appointed man, whether he belong to the church or not.

The laws of gravitation, the laws of attraction and repulsion, and the law of chemical affinity, are all a part of God's laws, and nature, by its action, is simply revealing them to the intelligent mind. The idea of condemning a man to prison because he discovered that the earth revolved around the sun should be justly followed by imprisoning the God who made it to do so. The evolution of matter from one stage to another is only the process by which the infinite mind outworks its purpose..

Science goes back to the time when worlds were gathered together in one seething mass gyrating in space and, in the process of time, shows how they were thrown off and built up. Science, again, marks different epochs through which this planet has passed until it has reached its present stage of physical development. Theologians talk of the creation of the world out of nothing six thousand years ago, and modern science proves, from the world itself, that it has always been in existence, and takes you back in its history twelve thousand, and even twenty thousand years. So much the better for science, and so much the worse for theology. That science has not yet found an individualized spirit in man does not argue that it will not, nor prevent all that which it has demonstrated in the realms of natural science from becoming a part of, and an important factor in, the building up of a comprehensive philosophy which shall take in all the various branches of knowledge, and strengthen, rather than weaken, man's understanding of, and reverence for, the deity and his attributes. Then we shall no longer have trials for heresy, or the arraignment of one opinion against another. Each will strive to attain unto the heights beyond, and will be too much occupied in the pursuit of truth, to quarrel with the other. Demonstrations of all claims made, will be as much demanded within, as they are now sought for without, the domain of religion. Nor will the religion of the future be relegated to a sphere essentially apart from all earthly interests; it will be, instead, the silver thread running through all forms of truth and holding them together in one continuous chain which, beginning with God, loses itself only in the vast realms of eternity.

Spiritualism holds that the world is the body of God and that the life is the soul of God, and wherein it fails to comprehend it hesitates to condemn.

Do Spiritualists Believe in God?

In the universal God, yes; in the theological interpretation, no; as the orthodox God, no. Every man makes a God about as large as he is himself; when you know him you will know the God he believes in. The more cruel the nature and ignorant the mind, the more revengeful the God; the more liberal the mind and loving the heart, the more beneficent the God.

Spiritualists believe in no direct action or intervention of the divine mind, against or contrary to his divine law, and, therefore, advisory prayers, such as asking for rain, fair weather and bountiful crops, are foolish and inconsistent.

Anger is a human but not a divine attribute, and God, through the law of compensation, confers upon each human being whatsoever is his, regardless of the religious beliefs or mental attitude of that individual. The idea of reconciling God to man, and making an investment through the instrumentality of the church which will pay a good return in time and eternity, is inconsistent with all that is thus far known of the action of spiritual law. The effort being to reconcile the lower man to the higher man and bring all the warring material elements into accord with the action of the superior self.

The orthodox God, so it is said, ordered men and women to be burned alive, massacres of all kinds, and the final condemnation of the majority of the human race to eternal punishment. The spiritualist's God is a supreme presence whereby all things ultimately work together for good, and what the highest has attained is held in possibility by the lowest.

Do Spiritualists Believe in the Bible?

As the word of the supreme spirit, no. But it is such a compendium of ideas as would be expected to emanate from the orthodox Jehovah, who claims the honor of its authorship. But there are no less than twenty-seven different bibles in the world, each claiming the divine authority; and whether you turn to the sacred books of India or Persia, or to the revelations made by John Smith or Brigham Young, there is about as much evidence in one as in the other of divine authorship. In fact, the much-condemned Mormons of Salt Lake City are but following in the footsteps of King David and King Solomon, who, in the halcyon days of the christian bible, were said to be men after God's own heart, and compared to lilies of the field.

The bibles of all countries are, in reality, a phase of the history of the different people who inhabited them, and in these histories earthly and spiritual events are presented in such a heterogeneous way that it becomes difficult, now, to separate one from the other. The christian bible, which we presume is the one referred to, presents more striking contrasts than all the others put together; it is inconsistent with the demonstrations of nature, repeatedly contradicts itself, and, yet, through the new testament, particularly, there is a line of thought suggested which is both elevating and encouraging. No lover of the truth can fail to see this, and if the life of Jesus was carefully edited it would present a lesson of incalculable value to mankind.

But God, the universal spirit, speaks to every age in the development of that age, and His bible is found not on the printed pages of any one volume, but in the universal book of nature which every day is revealing new truths for the benefit of the entire world.

Do Spiritualists Believe in the Devil?

The idea that there is a personality of evil, well-nigh supreme in his power, who was once an angel of light, but is now roaming over the earth seeking whom he may devour, was one that found ready acceptance up to the early part of the present century. Sometimes a snake, often a lion, and always an enemy. This monster, whose residence was in hell, but whose presence pervaded the entire world, was greatly dreaded and feared. He was a necessary factor in the theological scheme. Without a devil a savior would be a superfluity and, consequently, children of all ages were taught of his existence and feared him accordingly. Of late years, this idea has undergone much modification, not because there has been any new revelation in regard to it, but because thinkers outside the church have educated those inside, and shown the fallaciousness of the idea. Albeit the thought of his existence still shadows the human mind, and it plays as important, if not as prominent, a one in the theological scheme as ever.

The spiritualist has done more to modify the power of the devil than almost any one else. He holding that if God be supreme, whatever exists, either in heaven or earth, does so as the result of that supremacy; and that evil is simply undeveloped good, which later on will be made to serve the purposes of heaven. The devil is a man of straw, built out of the ignorance and superstitions of a foolish mind, and destroyed by every revelation that nature makes.

Do Spiritualists Believe in a Savior?

Man surrounded by the action of laws which he has not the ability to understand, constantly feels his own insufficiency. He reaches out, as a child does, for something whereby to guide himself, and, face to face with the great mystery of death, he instinctively searches for some mediator in the great unknown. It is for this reason that the theologians have been able to make acceptable the theory of redemption through the blood of Jesus. It is also flattering to the egotism of man to be taught that God took upon himself human form, lived, suffered and died to save unborn millions from his own wrath. Having created man exactly as he is, and foreordained him to become whatever he may be, it is only natural that he should seek to mitigate his sufferings in every way.

But there is probably no subject extant concerning which so much nonsense has been written and sung as this one of Jesus and salvation. Indeed the most fabled tales of childhood hours sink into insignificance before their grotesque stupidity. "Believe and ye shall be saved; believe not and ye shall be damned," while all the time belief is not dependent upon either the will, nor yet, the inclination of the individual.

Salvation means that Jesus and his blood furnishes an escape from just punishment for sins committed. But a higher and grander religion would teach man to meet the angel of retribution and accept whatever penalty his misdeeds merited and, through learning the lesson that such punishment contains, be freed from the baneful influences of unholy desires, and compel him to recognize that a confession of sins, and a profession of religion, followed by a transgression of nature's law, could only result in disaster to the individual, and eventual destruction to society; while, if he walks, hand in hand, with nature, and fulfils her behests, professions would be superfluous, and confession unnecessary. Knowledge, then, will have taken the place of faith, and those who walk in the light of her sweet presence, take no uncertain steps, her power transcending all others, and outliving all, save time itself.

Every man becomes his own savior the moment he ceases to do evil and learns to do well. Jesus of Nazareth, by the simplicity of his life, his noble devotion to what he considered to be true, his wide sympathy and lofty aspirations, furnishes an example of what it is possible for man to attain unto. In this sense, he is a savior so far as his life becomes an encouragement to others, and in no other way.

Do Spiritualists Believe in Heaven and Hell?

Spiritualists hold that there is a spiritual world into which every spirit passes, when its work on earth is completed, that heaven and hell, instead of being localities, are states within rather than conditions without, and that death has nothing whatever to do with the realization of either. He who is in accord with himself may be in a world of contention, but he has heaven within. He who is at discord with himself, no matter how fair the external surroundings, has, so long as that discord remains, a hell within himself. Dying only takes the spirit from one condition to another and there emphasizes spiritual states. It is as if man's real spiritual development had been placed in the scales, weighed and then, by a law of spiritual gravitation, rises or falls according to its own inherent qualities. The reward or punishment, of which so much is said, is the result of the decision as to what that state shall be. It is dependent upon the interior life of the spirit and upon absolutely nothing else, it being remembered, always, that a man can never get away from himself and that in the spiritual world disguise is impossible. Each spirit stands forth for exactly what it is. The good are attracted to the spheres of light and find their happiness, not in decking themselves out in flowing robes and shining crowns, but in the contemplation of still grander achievements, while the bad are continually in the presence of their own evil doings which are apparent to all.

Progress, despite the orthodox church, is as universal after death as before, and no spirit is ever left in the world of outer darkness until the star of hope has been placed in the heavens above him.

Theories of infant damnation, eternal punishment and everlasting misery, together with the picture of heavenly joys, as taught by the church, find no acceptance, whatever, at the hands of the intelligent spiritualist.

Do Spiritualists Believe in Prayer?

Yes, they do; but they do not believe in man's thanking God for everything that is in the world, and in the same breath suggesting an amendment and a change thereof. They do not believe that God will ever change one of his laws, which being his, are founded upon absolute justice, though all the world should unite in one common prayer. At the same time they hold that the concentration of the mind upon desired points, brings the individual spirit into relationship with the law, whereby it is possible of accomplishment, and also attracts other spirit intelligencies, who add their influence to the same purposes. Prayers, however, should have a spiritual, rather than a material tendency, and when uttered in the spirit of true desire, cannot fail to produce a harmonizing and beneficial effect upon the individual.

Are There Evil Spirits?

This has been the bugbear that has opposed the demonstration of any spiritual power throughout all the centuries. Very few church people deny the facts of spiritualism. They hold it is possible that spirits may manifest themselves upon the earth, but that all such spirits are of evil origin and, if not in direct partnership with the devil himself, are allied thereto; that they are spirits who are not good enough for heaven, and not yet bad enough for hell, so they remain, for a time, in outer darkness, awaiting their final punishment and, meantime, amuse themselves by deceiving mankind. So cunning are these evil spirits that they may deceive the elect of heaven, and the more plausible and reasonable they appear the more deceptive they are.

The spiritual world is made up of the men and women who have lived in this world, and as sin and vice have been relatives since time began, it is not at all surprising that those who have died steeped to the core with sin should, on their return to the earth, manifest the same evil tendencies. But, at the same time, such spirits only return when there is something in the individual to attract them, and those who wish for the presence of the good, the wise and the true, have only to worship at the shrine of goodness, wisdom and truth to receive them. However, suppose that evil spirits do return more frequently even than good ones, that would serve quite as well to prove man's continued life after death.

*　*　*　*　*　*

In short, modern spiritualism holds that after death the identity of the human spirit is preserved, and that, under proper conditions, through certain sensitive organizations, such demonstrations of that life can be given as to prove it conclusively.

Mediums are persons possessed of an organization differing from the rest of mankind, inasmuch as the extremes are more highly marked and the entire nervous system more attuned to the emotional than to the logical. Through these mouth-pieces the spirits of the departed have, in all ages of the world, been able to manifest themselves with more or less intelligence, governed, to a great degree, by the conditions whereby such communications were made possible. Sometimes Jesus of Nazareth, Moses, Confucius, Joan of Arc, and other rarely gifted natures, have shone down upon the darkness of the human mind with a force and power born, alone, of divine inspiration. It was not that their minds were particularly gifted by any system of education, or process of enfoldment, but that their organizations, both physical and spiritual, were so in attune to the unuttered law of heaven, that they voiced its word, and later times interpreted and comprehended its meaning. Not to their own age was the message given, not to their own time was the word spoken, for the age rewarded them, invariably, with persecution and death; but the age that came after got the fuller meaning, clasped hands with the thought given, and sought to follow whithersoever it led. Not the less credit is given them because they were instruments in the hands of the spiritual world, rather than originators of the thoughts, possibly more is due them, since, had they not been fitting and worthy instruments, the words would have remained unsaid.

In Part X, we shall speak of the various phases of mediumship far more extensively than we are able to do here, since there it is classified and explained.

Be it understood, that spiritualism rests upon the direct evidence of its truth, which has been given and continues to be given, in the present day. What a man sees he is bound to believe, and all the cries of evil spirits, delusion and fraud, have no effect upon a mind that has convinced itself through actual proof and demonstration.

PART X.

Mediumship and Spiritual Phenomena.

Forms of Mediumship.

Remarks upon Mediumship.

Mediumship and Spiritual Phenomena.

(Entered according to Act of Congress, in the year 1893, by AUGUSTA W. FLETCHER, M. D., in the office of the Librarian of Congress at Washington.)

It would be impossible to proceed in the consideration of the subject before us, without referring to the spiritual phenomena which have marked this age with singular significance, as they have many a former one. The phenomena are important, not so much for what they demonstrate as for the line of thought and spiritual possibility which they suggest. This has been, perhaps, the first time in human experience that these strange occurrences, now so common, have every reason to demand the credence of the wise, and the careful consideration and investigation of the studious; but this is an age when the spirit of inquiry is abroad, when prejudice and superstition have, to a great degree, succumbed to the advancing power of intelligent thought, and, perforce, the mind goes out, untrammeled, into the domain of natural philosophy, seeking to prove all things, and holding fast to that which is true. It is peculiar, in an age marked for its atheistical tendencies, when doubts are everywhere, and beliefs have scarcely a place to rest their feet, that there should be any particular interest in spiritual things, which are, in fact, the antithesis of materialistic inquiry. However, such is the case, and, despite the teachings of natural science and the scoffing of men of learning, there is a large and considerable following of intelligent minds who are able to pass beyond the boundary line of a personal, physical existence and stand, face to face, with that higher form of life which follows in its train. These persons call themselves spiritualists, in the extreme sense of the word; but, all the same, they are journeying toward the same centre by another and, possibly, less direct road.

All ages of the world have been blessed by evidences of a continued life; some of these have been varied and marked in character, and, hundreds of years after, have served as a foundation for a new system of religious belief, as, for instance, the spiritual demonstrations that are recorded in the bible, and which extend throughout the entire range of human experience, from the rolling of the stone away from the door of the sepulchre to the translating of Elijah in a chariot of fire. In later time, similar powers have been possessed by individuals, which their own age did not accept with as friendly an interpretation; but, inspired by a stupid superstition, sought to crush out, by all sorts of iniquitous punishments, that which they were unable to understand or appreciate. The Salem witchcraft, in which we find an illustration of the presence of spiritual power, marks an epoch in the history of civilization which, to-day, excites the pity of the world.

Forty-five years ago, in the little house at Hydesville, N. Y., the quiet of the home was broken by the attempt of spirits to prove their existence in the spiritual world. Two little children, members of the Fox family, were said to be the instrument through which this demonstration was given. So powerful were the efforts of these spirits, that the attention of the family, and, later on, the community, was enlisted, and furnished men of science, theologians and the world at-large, with a subject for discussion. Opinions were expressed with more vehemence than intelligence, and were as divergent as it is possible to imagine. At first, the whole matter was declared to be a humbug, a common, flimsy trick devised to entrap the weak-minded; in fact, the doctors, and many of the clergymen, openly asserted that the raps produced in the presence of these children, were simply the result of the action of their knee and toejoints; but while this might explain the production of the sounds, it in no way furnished a reason for the intelligence and knowledge which they conveyed. Then they took the other horn of the dilemma, these self-appointed critics, and as vociferously declared that all the occurrences were due to the action of some subtle law in magnetism and electricity. What these two elements were these wise men failed to explain, and, because so little was known of these forces, their assertions seemed the more profound. But here they were met by the intelligence conveyed, for which they offered no direct explanation, and the more enlightened gradually dropped the subject altogether. The theologians, however, realizing that if this thing grew in strength and power their own citadel would be in danger, persisted in their denunciation; but ended, finally, in declaring that the devil, who is supposed to be at the bottom of all of the mischief in this world, had chosen this method of deceiving mankind for its ultimate destruction; and, as the devil has always been renowned for being one of the most clever and able personalities extant, herein was found an explanation for all that had occurred. By this time, however, the subject had spread from Maine to Oregon, had crossed the ocean, and was enlisting the attention of the crowned heads of Europe and the East, and, during the past forty-five years, has continued to grow until it pervades nearly every department of human life. In art, literature and modern science it holds an important place, and, to-day, the younger and more liberal class of theologians are inducting its teachings into the theological system, and looking for its demonstrations to prove, in a universal sense, what they, in a more limited one, have been asserting for years. These manifestations have adapted themselves to every human requirement, and whether it be the rapping upon or the tipping of tables, the writing of messages by spirit power, the seeing of faces, trance-speaking or materialization (which is the taking on, temporarily, of physical elements by the spirits), the object and purpose have been the same, namely, to prove that after death the spiritual man continues to live.

A medium is one who furnishes peculiar magnetic elements through which spiritual demonstrations, of whatever character or kind, are given. His moral character, mental development and social position, have nothing whatever to do with his ability in this direction. That they may have something to do with the character of the manifestation is true; but some form could be given, whether he be morally good or bad. It is the organization, not the man, temperament and not education, peculiar, physical, magnetic quality rather than mental development. Thus a man may be bad as a man, and yet be remarkable as a medium. This, in the same degree, is true of a man gifted in any particular line. He may be a great artist and create results which will live centuries after he is individually forgotten, and yet not be a great moral teacher. He may invent wonderful mechanical appliances which will be of untold benefit to the world, and yet be a liar and a thief. He, like Byron, George Eliot, or George Sand, may be of more than ordinary genius and yet scarcely an individual that one would set up as a pattern for the rest of the world to model after. Mediumship is a gift as much as is the inspiration of the poet or the genius of the artist.

Physical Mediums.

This, perhaps, is the most common, comprehensive and conclusive form that has yet been vouchsafed. By physical mediumship we mean the ability of spirits to produce physical results through acting upon, or in conjunction with, material objects. Raps, the moving of furniture, the production of lights and spirit faces in the darkness, are all evidences of the possession of this power. Through them, ideas, thoughts and messages are conveyed, from the spiritual world to the earth plane, in much the same way that a message is telegraphed from one city to another, the spirit being the intelligent operator at the other end of the line. This power is usually revealed through the sitting at a table alone, or in connection with others, for the specific purpose of seeing what will happen. After two or three attempts, perhaps at the very first, the table will begin to move, and, through calling over the alphabet, which is responded to by the oscillations of the table, messages are spelled out and much direct information given. This information will consist in giving names of the disembodied who may be present, advice and comments upon earthly affairs, and other suggestions of a character that will betray the identity of those making such communications. It must be remembered that the mental attitude of those forming the circle for such investigation, will have more to do with the nature and character of the communications than anything else. Frivolity and irreverence serve to attract spirits who, when on earth, were of like nature and characteristics.

A physical medium is of a very emotional temperament, however perfectly developed, and is more susceptible to physical influences than any other class of mediums. Consequently, after a seance of this kind, his material associations should be guarded against, as, through the loss of magnetism, he has become much more amenable to all kinds of passing influences which infest the air, and he may, possibly, aye, very likely will, succumb to some of them. Enough attention has never been paid to the conditions surrounding a medium directly after the exhibition of his power; for, through the indiscriminate commingling of different magnetisms, a large number of the disasters which follow on the train of an ignorant exercise of his power is due. He should immediately pass into the company of friends, who, instead of going over the seance or, in fact, talking about it at all, should swing to the other extreme and introduce some light form of amusement, and, possibly later on, he should take some refreshment. But great care should be taken to avoid the use of any stimulating or intoxicating drinks, since, while in his sensitive state, some of the spirits possessed of debasing tendencies may rush into his sphere and, by exerting a subtle influence, induce him to do things which, in an exactly normal condition, he would regret.

It is well to state here that every medium is under the guidance and control of two or more distinct bands of spirits who have the manifestations in charge, both for their production and direction. The spirits producing physical manifestations through the instrumentality of any medium are not advanced spirits, but are in close relationship with earthly forces and are able to affinitize themselves therewith by the effort of their will. At the same time, they are responsive to a band of spirit-chemists who work in consonance with them, and direct, to a great degree, the purposes of their work, in like manner as the contractor directs the labor of those whom he employs. But these spirits are not always directly connected with their medium, and are, sometimes, unable to counteract adverse influences, consequently, results follow which, were they all powerful, they would, without doubt, prevent. Then, again, while a man may be magnetically and particularly well adapted for their use, in this direction, he may be mentally opposed to it. and his ignorance and intention place many obstacles in the way, for the more perfect outworking of the original design. This must always be the case until some one shall arise who will make the laws of mediumship a study, and then the medium, before he enters in upon a public career, will be so educated as to intelligently discriminate between those conditions which will assist and those which will mar the result. He will be able to decide when everything is working together for good, using his powers only when everything is at its best. He will thus be able to prevent the numbers of partial failures which, in the present state of ignorance, excite so much unfriendly comment. As it is, the ordinary medium, although possessed of extraordinary gifts, perhaps knows as little of the laws governing their exercise as does the casual observer. A school of mediumship is a necessity for the best and highest results to be assured.

Trance Mediumship.

By far the most common, valuable and highly appreciated form of mediumship, is that where the medium's brain is either taken full possession of, or so held, hypnotically, by the power of a spirit, as to obliterate, for the time being, the individuality of the medium, and make him the vehicle for the transmission of the thoughts, ideas and wishes of the controlling intelligences. While under an influence or control of this kind, information of great value and interest has been given, such as names, events and advice, wholly outside the knowledge or the known capacity of the medium himself. There seems to be an intensification of all his powers; for, at that time, he is more perceptive, intuitive and sympathetic than when in a purely normal state. Not infrequently he is clairvoyant and clairaudient; paints pictures, writes books and composes music; all of which is as wonderful to him afterward, as it is remarkable to others. But this class of mediumship, more than any other, is the victim of the embodied and disembodied. If the medium is subject to the influence of a spirit, how much more likely is he to be affected by the character of those about him. Strong minds in the body may take control of his brain, instead of the spirit intelligences; thus he may become the mouth-piece of their thoughts, rather than an instrument in the hands of the spiritual world. Such persons, who must be of a highly sensitive order, cannot come under the same line of human criticism and judgment, as is applied to those in every-day life; and yet, not infrequently, they are subject to a more severe and rigorous one. Conditions that would not affect a blacksmith or a wheelwright, would mar, very much, the work of the poet or the artist and, admitting the existence of spiritual mediumship, certainly the conditions surrounding a medium, should be considered with equal care and attention.

Contrary to the conditions which govern physical mediumship, the mental development of trance mediums has a great deal to do with the results obtained through them. The old idea of the bigger the fool the better the medium, has been proven to be both fallacious and untenable. The spiritual world creates nothing, it simply brings into active use that which is. The medium is like a musical instrument; if he be uneducated and inexperienced, there may be only one or two octaves that will give forth sound; but if he be educated, has had experience, and his nature is rounded out, he becomes an instrument where all the notes respond to the touch of the master's hand.

Theo. Parker could never express himself to his own satisfaction, save through a mental organization that was correspondingly developed with his own. The more education a medium can have, the greater his psychic capacity, and the more perfect channel will he become for the transmission of thought. Education, in the true sense of the word, is to the mind what proper exercise is to the body.

The first evidence of the possession of trance mediumship, is found in the ability to obtain quick mental impressions, sensing conditions belonging to individuals with whom one is brought in contact, and, in seasons of quiet, experiencing a loss of one's external consciousness. These conditions can be emphasized by appropriating an hour in each day, which should be devoted to their development. Two or three congenial friends, in sympathy with this object, should join hands around a table, and, avoiding all unfriendly discussion preceding the hour, concentrate their minds upon the purpose desired. The time may then be passed in seeking spiritual help. Sometimes the hand of the sensitive will be used automatically, sometimes impressions may be first made upon the brain and then written out, or a heaviness will pass over him, which will finally be followed by partial or complete entrancement, which, if persisted in, will result favorably to all concerned; but, during the first months of incipient mediumship, too much credence must not be given to what is said through its influence, as the imperfect conditions and incomplete development will make it well-nigh impossible, no matter how good the intention of the spirit, to transmit his thought with any exactitude. You have to know, to become acquainted with, the controlling spirits, just the same as you do with individuals upon the earth. Death does not destroy, it only modifies mental peculiarities; and hate, love, truth, falsehood, right and wrong are as apparent, if less active, upon the spiritual as upon the earthly plane of existence. Not every spirit will be self-sacrificing and disinterested in the advice given, and it should become a matter of deep consideration, to the thoughtful, as to how best discriminate between the wise and the unwise, the good and the bad. After a certain epoch is passed, however, and the control of advanced spirits assured, mediumship of this form will continue on the even tenor of its way, and be developed to a state of great value and reliability. Then the thoughts of inspired speakers, and teachings received in the seance room, can be accepted as being what they purport to be; not truth in the absolute sense, perhaps, but a greater degree of truth than mortals are able to obtain through purely earthly sources. Yet, through these evidences of the control of spirits, will be found the peculiarities of the medium upon which such control is exercised. This is invariably true, and must always be taken into consideration, more or less. It becomes much wiser, then, in consulting a medium, to allow the controlling spirits to conduct the communications unaided, since talking the matter over with the medium, either before or after, may serve to develop a prejudice which is liable to tincture much that he may say while under such influence. This was particularly true of Emanuel Swedenborg, who was one of the most remarkable mediums of his time. His early theological training, without doubt, colored much of that which he wrote. Had he been devoid of such religious training he would have put a far different interpretation upon that which was given him by the spiritual world, and which he has recorded for the benefit of the generations that were to follow.

Healing Mediumship.

A class of almost unrecognized workers in the world is known as healing mediums. They are persons not unlike physical mediums in temperament, but with a different application of the magnetic power that surrounds them. In the former, the spirit-band seeks to produce demonstrations of a different kind, and uses this power for that purpose; but, in the latter, the power is applied for the amelioration of physical suffering and the building up of the physical organization. Such mediums are surrounded by strong magnetic auras which are ever present with them whithersoever they go. It may not, however, be in operation; in fact, it rarely ever is, unless under the direction of a controlling band who seem to be carrying on a work for humanity which they began in their earthly life, and are now endeavoring to continue through this agency. The controlling spirits, under this phase of work, are almost invariably physicians, who seem to have found, in this adaptation of magnetic laws, more ability to alleviate human suffering than through the administering of drugs and medicines. While controlling, these spirits are able to attract from the atmosphere and individuals whatever magnetism they require and then to envelop the sufferer with it, until, through the laws of adaptability, it becomes a part of himself. Many remarkable cures have been made in this way, but the article upon Mental Healers (Part IV.) will furnish elaboration of the subject.

INSPIRATIONAL MEDIUMSHIP.

Few persons are aware of how much their life and work is affected by either the direct or indirect influence of departed spirits, who, from their very nature, are bound to be more or less concerned in the affairs of earth for a long time after they have withdrawn from the stage of its activities. The purposes, hopes and ambitions of a lifetime are not ended when the spirit ceases its connection with external life, but remain after death, sometimes strengthened and intensified, and seek some organization in the earth through which to carry them out. Sometimes a spirit of strongly developed individuality will, directly after death, associate himself with a person still living, whose mental capacity is not dissimilar to his own, and follow that person through the rest of his earthly career. He will constantly impress him with thoughts and suggestions which, when carried out, are bound to result successfully. Or, again, a spirit may be attracted to a number of different embodied personalities more or less similar to his own and, in certain departments of his work, become the all controlling power, although not taking the slightest interest in the general life of the individual. A man deeply engaged in a certain reformatory work, to which he has, in a great measure, devoted his life, is called to the spiritual world before he sees the fruition of his endeavors. He has left his associates here in the world who, with equal zeal, forward to completion that which he has left unfinished. To suppose that he could instantly forget the nature of that work, and pass into a state of restful oblivion, is to ignore the character of the true reformer. He who has sacrificed, on the altar of truth, much of the happiness that life held, is not likely to permit himself to be absorbed in joy and pleasure while those purposes, perhaps, are still in an embryonic state. He is still attracted to the old centre of his activities, but is interested, only, in the work that he began and to which he gave his life, and will immediately connect himself with one or more of his former co-workers and continue to co-operate with them so long as there is any necessity for so doing. Many speakers on the public platform who are, at times, marvelously eloquent and, at other times, when judged by their best efforts, mediocre, are persons subject to momentary inspirations and, during outbursts of oratory, become the channel through which some spirit is pouring out his thoughts. All persons who are intensely in earnest are subject to such inspiration. They do not know whence it comes; in fact, are frequently surprised at the result and, at such times, are said to be at their best. This inspiring power is not confined to any one department of life, but relates to every phase wherein individuals are enough engrossed, in the subject of the moment, to forget themselves and give their best strength to their work. What is called good judgment wherein, as is often the case, judgment could not enter at all, is simply an impression received from some spirit friend, whose keener perceptions are able to foresee results which are not within the range of human vision. All persons are subject to these intimations much more than they are aware of, and many pass by unnoticed what might be a strong evidence of some presence outside of their own, who is seeking to guide them along the troubled way of life. And this does not relate to what is commonly called imagination, nor is it our desire to stimulate that unhealthy state of dependence whereby any individual should rely upon outside help altogether, for that help is only valuable and, in fact, only to be relied upon when the individual has done the very best he could for himself.

Speaking of the continuance of work by a spirit, calls to mind an example which would illustrate this idea to the understanding of all:

An author-critic of considerable ability, and especially enthusiastic in his work, passed out into the spiritual world, leaving his daughter, a young lady of about twenty, well-nigh alone. She became very much straitened in circumstances and, about that time there was published a book which excited a great amount of comment. It was just such a work as her father, with his clear acumen, would have been able to deal with, successfully. Sitting alone, in the old library, where he had worked for so many years, she fell to thinking of him, when, impulsively, she drew out a drawer, in the secretary, which contained a large number of quills, it being a peculiarity of his to preserve all of the pens which he had used in his literary work. She took them out and placed them on the table before her, thinking of the hand, now vanished, that had guided them across the pages, implanting thereon suggestions and ideas that had done much to mould and shape the thoughts of the world. The volume, aforesaid, lay upon the table beside the pens; the fire burned low, and all was still throughout the house. Musing, for a time, upon the thoughts suggested by the room and its associations, she felt, rather than saw, the presence of her father. Instinctively, she reached across the table, took up one of the quills, and placed a pad of paper before her. The next morning her mother found her sitting in the library. A large pile of manuscript lay before her, in her father's handwriting, which, on being sent to the publisher, was declared to be in his own elegant form of composition. Subsequently, on many other occasions, covering a space of years, the same thing was repeated, although in and of herself she was unable to write with more than ordinary intelligence. The explanation of all this, from a worldly stand-point, is difficult, but, from a spiritual one, quite the reverse, since, thinking deeply of her father, she had attracted him to the room filled with his thoughts and permeated with his magnetism; thus he was able to come into direct, spiritual relationship with his child, and inspire her mind to write whatsoever he wished, he, without doubt, taking more interest in the production of the work than those who gained the benefit thereafter.

Actors upon the stage may be so intensely identified with the part that they attract the very historical characters they represent, or, if not, some greater interpreter of human emotions, who may add his influence to their own. These artists are usually of a highly emotional nature, and, in such great undertakings, are wholly incapacitated for social relationship.

William Lloyd Garrison insisted that he constantly felt the presence of John Brown during all the latter years of his work in the cause of freedom, and Mrs. Browning, in writing to a friend, said, "the external evidences of spiritual life, I know little of, but there are continual interior impressions, and suggestions, that could come from no other source, and, to me, are most suggestive and conclusive."

Warnings, which are frequently being received of events to occur, some of ill-fortune and some of good, are also the result of spirit inspiration. A man about to take a railway train is, for some inexplicable reason, seized with a desire not to do so. He returns home, and, the next morning, reads that the train met with a severe accident. His action is explicable only from the spiritual stand-point, wherein it is shown that some spirit friend saw the danger, and kept him out of it.

Dreams are often nothing more or less than visitations from the spiritual world; the body, being far more sensitive when in repose, allows a freer action to the individual spirit, and makes such impressions possible. In short, if man would carefully study himself, he would find that the spiritual world envelops him, and that which he receives, mentally and spiritually, is but the result of its action.

MATERIALIZATION.

Materialization is the power by which a disembodied spirit is enabled to temporarily reclothe itself in material form, so as to appear like unto its former earthly embodiment. Impossible as this may seem to be, thousands of well-authenticated facts could, if necessary, be adduced. The ghost who haunts the church-yard at night, or flits by, with noiseless tread, over the stairway, is a modified form of materialization. There are three particular factors in the production of this form of manifestation: the medium, the investigators, and last, but not least, the operating spirits. The medium is usually separated from the investigators, by a perfectly dark cabinet, which serves as a workshop for the spirits. The medium is the magnetic centre from which the controls draw a large amount of the elements used. The investigators are seated in a semi-dark room, and furnish, also, some of the magnetic qualities that are employed in the production of the manifestations. It will be seen, therefore, that there should be as little dissimilarity of temperament and mind as possible among them. Singing is usually indulged in, so that the company may be brought into more or less accord, and, in a short time, magnetic relations are established between them and the spirits in the cabinet workshop. One discordant nature, however, will be sufficient to destroy the entire result, and persons of a highly nervous or emotional temperament, or those suffering from any physical disease, should not sit in seances of this kind. Their condition would affect and disturb the manifestations, and, although gaining for themselves, physically, a temporary stimulus from the momentary excitement, they would, in reality, lose their own strength and power in the end. After sitting quietly for a few moments the spirit chemists are able to draw from the medium, the sitters, and the atmosphere, a certain amount of magnetic force, which they are enabled, at will, to precipitate, and under their manipulation it becomes a solid body. The elements composing this body are used by all the spirits appearing at the seance. The moment that one spirit has materialized outside the cabinet, and, in a measure, accomplished the purpose of his coming, he returns, and instantly the body is disintegrated, awaiting the impulse of some other spirit to reform itself into human shape again, and so on, and on, until there have been known to appear as many as twenty-five or thirty fully formed materializations in an hour. Not that there were any new magnetic elements employed after the first materialization, but that those which had already been collected were remoulded, by the will of the manifesting spirits, into such shape and form as would best express their purpose.

That all spirits will bear some likeness to the medium is to be expected, since, from that source, as we have said, the larger amount of the elements used are supplied. It will be seen that a cabinet is a necessity, since light is a positive element and would have an unfavorable effect upon the negative influences, for the same reason that a photographer must develop his plate in a dark room before it will stand the light. It would be impossible to precipitate the magnetic wave, referred to, except under the most negative condition.

In these manifestations the spirits take on forms largely resembling their earthly ones, it being a law that spirits returning to matter shall take on a like condition to that which governed them when leaving the material world. Thus, peculiarities of form, figure and speech are represented with wonderful clearness and exactness. The bible student will find in the return of Jesus, after his death, a parallel to all this. The seance in the upper chamber resulted in a materialization of Jesus of Nazareth. The onlookers accepted it as such, save one, who would not believe his own eyes, and demanded that some proof, other than that offered, should be given him. He, therefore, was called to the spirit, placed his fingers upon the wounded side and hand, and thus his doubts were dispelled; at which the spirit gave utterance to these memorable words, which contain the gist of a great spiritual law:

"Blessed are ye who have seen and believe, but more blessed are ye who have not seen and yet believe."

Which interpreted, from a spiritual stand-point, is that those who see are convinced through and by the physical senses only, while those who are possessed of spiritual development are able to intuitively apprehend the truth without physical or ocular demonstration.

And this brings us to the subject of test conditions, which has been a mooted question ever since the attempt to prove a continued life was undertaken. Various devices and clumsy contrivances have been applied to mediums to prevent fraud, which, if the investigator himself had been spiritually unfolded, would have been wholly unnecessary. Ropes, chains and handcuffs were put upon mediums with the idea of preventing them from practicing any deception, forgetting that the very state of mind that would induce the investigator to use such means for protection would militate against, if not absolutely prevent, any spiritual result. Later, an extraordinary invention, called the wire-cage, has been introduced, with somewhat varying results, it being held that if the medium was locked in the wire compartment whatever occurred outside that compartment would be satisfactory proof of the genuineness of the materialization. None of these devices have been operated with any great degree of success. In England, where physical mediumship is, in some of its phases, more marked than in America, more careful scientific tests have been applied than elsewhere. Prof. Crooks, F. R. S., applying the electrical test with the register attachment upon Florence Cook, was able to demonstrate her respirations even, and yet the manifestations went on precisely the same.

Some of the unfavorable results of all this testing is the spirit of curiosity that it develops in the mind of the investigator, and the low order of spirits that it attracts. Surely there ought to be and there is a better way of proving immortality than by resorting to handcuffs, ropes and locked wire-cages, which, from the very outset, presupposes that the medium is a trickster, only waiting for an opportunity to ply his trade. It is not from the means of protection against fraud that any honest conclusion should be made, but it is from the judgment of results, after every condition has been complied with, that the truth will be found. The evidence of the reality of this manifestation will be found in the personalities of the spirits, and the information that they impart, rather than by or through any other means. Mediums desiring to obtain the best results should discriminate as to the individuals they admit to their seances.

A form of mediumship, known as transfiguration, will account for many of the perplexing demonstrations that force themselves upon the attention of the investigator, and relieves the honest medium from a trying situation, wherein even personal integrity as well as mediumship itself is called in question. By this we mean that when the cabinet spirits are enabled to disassociate the magnetic wave, referred to, from the sphere of the medium, or to gain, from other sources, all the direct elements required for the production of independent materialization, these will, upon occasions, take possession of the body of the medium, change every line of his face and figure, and bring him out of the cabinet, and, while under control, personate first one spirit and then another, carrying the idea that the manifestation is what it purports to be and never, by suggestion or otherwise, leading those present to understand that it is other than the direct spiritual embodiment. The possibility of this will be evident to any person who has ever studied the subject in the least degree, and, while irritating beyond expression, is none the less a fact, which compels recognition; for, if a spirit has the power to entrance the brain and speak through a medium, it will have the power to make that medium responsive to his will, and, being desirous of coming into connection with earthly friends, will use every means in his power to accomplish that end. When such is the case, no attention must be paid to anything save the information conveyed, since this manifestation is as much an evidence of spirit power as is any other; the only trouble being, that the conclusion the investigator is left to form, as to the means employed, is erroneous. This result occurs only when there is a partially developed condition of mediumship, wherein the higher guides have not obtained absolute control, and in the presence of strongly hypnotic persons, who persistently keep their minds in a state of positive activity. It is not an evidence, necessarily, of deceitful intention on the part of the medium. It is probably the best that can be done under the conditions furnished, and, in a further study of this subject, the possibility of providing better surrounding and more responsive elements will suggest itself.

"Is there not much fraud in mediumship on the part

MATERIALIZATION.

of those who assume powers of which they are not possessed?" is a question frequently asked.

Without doubt there is. It would be impossible to expect that in this age of the world spiritualism would be exempt from an element that pervades every other department of life. There are some people, without doubt, who have stolen the livery of heaven to serve the devil in, but they are sure to come to grief in a short time, and do comparatively little harm save to themselves. In the present chaotic state of the spiritualistic movement it is utterly impossible to have a careful classification, either of manifestations or laws, upon which results depend.

Remarks upon Mediumship.

(Entered according to Act of Congress, in the year 1893, by Augusta W. Fletcher, M. D., in the office of the Librarian of Congress at Washington.)

We hinted, in the previous article, that there should be a class of mediumship wherein the peculiarities of those possessed of psychic powers should become the subject of thought and consideration, and a line of study, or education, followed which should serve to unfold them to their fullest capacity. Up to the present moment those who are possessed of the power *happen* to have it. How it can be developed, and what is its intent and purpose, they know nothing at all about. They simply drift, carried along by the force of its current, approximating, only, the great good that might be accomplished by using their powers as a means of livelihood, on the one hand, or as a gratification of morbid curiosity on the other. We do not mean to say by this that there have not been men and women inspired by a great and noble motive in their work, but we do assert that the majority of mediums have not been able to move out of the sphere of their own personal exigencies, and that their mediumship was valuable only so far as it conduced to the accomplishment of personal ends. This must always be the case until the spiritualist more fully comprehends that he has something to do beside enjoy his religion, which means visiting mediums occasionally, now and then subscribing small sums to charities, but doing nothing for the upbuilding of the movement, or the promulgation of the truth. The Methodist, Baptist and Salvation Armyist are infinitely more interested in spreading their ideas broadcast than is the ordinary spiritualist, who, on Sunday, is more frequently found occupying the pew of some liberal church where the tendency is spiritualistic than in supporting meetings where his own ideas are taught and explained. In fact, with a few honorable exceptions, spiritualism, during the last half century, has rested upon the shoulders of its public mediums, who are expected to support themselves through their mediumship, or other avenues, and, in many cases, give their services for the benefit of societies, instead of receiving any direct benefit in return. This is in exact reversal of the system existing in other bodies, formed with like purposes in view. During the years of successful mediumship a medium is bound to receive attention and general support from the spiritualists, but, in a moment when, through untoward conditions, he makes a mistake, and his name catches the shadow, the outside world is more generous in its sympathies than are the spiritualists themselves. It would appear as if the spiritualists were willing to take all the glory, without bearing any of the responsibility.

This is particularly illustrated at the summer camp-meetings, where thousands of people act the part of zealous spiritualists, and take positions upon the governing boards, while at home, in their own town, they rarely, if ever, mention the subject, and their next door neighbors are not sure that they have ever heard of it.

Their excuse is that it might hurt their business, or their social position, which is a poor one when weighed against the value of the truth. At these camp meetings much good can be done when guided by intelligent minds in the body, who, in turn, would be assisted by intelligent minds out of the body. But, thus far, they have done little more than mix together balloon ascensions, skating rinks and spiritual manifestations, to the extent that the managers are more interested in catching each flying penny than in upbuilding the movement. Such places should be schools of spiritual thought, where serious minded people could go and, while enjoying the beauty of the natural scenery, study that most profound of philosophies, modern spiritualism. The best minds should be invited to appear, and both sides of all subjects receive a fair and dispassionate hearing. The platform should be governed by unprejudiced persons, and the personal animosities of an ignorant president should not be sufficient to stop any intelligent speaker. In fact, there appears to be two kinds of spiritualism, one which is conducted from a questionable position, with the spiritual world left out, and the other where there is an attempt to follow the teachings of the higher spirits. Wherever the latter is done the very best results follow, while the former is destined to end in chaos and disgrace. In admitting the possession of spiritual powers by any person the least that can be done is to give a respectful hearing to whatever is said, using it, or not, as the occasion and judgment shall decide; but some spiritualists seem to be willing to accept nothing, from the spiritual world even, unless it contains a reproduction of their own peculiar views. We remember, some years ago, being present at one of these out-of-door meetings when one of the most brilliant speakers and mediums that has ever graced the movement arose to give an address, under the control of his spirit guides. During the speech much needed and wholesome advice was administered to the management. No sooner had he finished than a man, who afterward proved to be an editor of a pseudo spiritualistic journal, rushed upon the platform, shook his fists in the face of the speaker and called his guides political liars. Strange to say, the president supported this ruffianly assailant, and the speaker was not allowed to appear again upon the platform. The wildest confusion ensued, and the audience, numbering thousands, left the auditorium angry and disgusted. Our position is, that the spiritualists should be at oneness with their mediums, that the interests of one are the interests of all, that there should be no selfish or party feeling, that the platform should be open to all who have a truth to speak, and that, instead of silencing one by force, kindly logic should be employed. Such is the counsel of those who are wise in the spiritual world.

If there could be a more careful classification of mediumistic powers, a more thoughtful study of the laws governing their use, and a closer affiliation, on the part of the spiritualists, with the work of the moment, many of the failures now so common would be avoided, and spiritualism would take its rightful place among the great educators of the world. The investigator would be able to learn where to find what he required, and the student would avoid that confusion of ideas which is brought about by the instruction received from unintelligent and unformed minds. The investigator of to-day often turns away entirely discouraged by the conflicting opinions of those from whom he is seeking information. So little, in fact, is known of the nature of mediumship that most public mediums find themselves, on the one hand, supported by a band of followers, and, on the other, pursued by another whose virulence is as deteriorating in its effect as the respect of friends is stimulating. And yet both classes call themselves spiritualists, and talk glibly enough about universal brotherhood and the glories of the harmoneal philosophy. When there shall be a legitimate organization among spiritualists, a standard of mediumship, and a comprehension of its laws and purposes, all these dangers will be avoided. But until that happy time, which seems almost utopian, things will move on in about the same channel as they formerly have done.

In the above we have but sought to give a timely suggestion. That it may disturb many to whom it applies is to be expected, but we feel that every unprejudiced mind will see its value and admit its justness.

We cannot leave the subject of mediumship without referring to many of the attempts to investigate, that have been made by societies and committees entirely outside of it. The report of the Seybert commission, for which the public looked with some interest, was as disappointing as it was non-conclusive. Without doubt Henry Seybert, when he was leaving his money to the University of Pennsylvania, for the establishing of a chair of philosophy which should devote a certain amount of time to the investigation of psychical subjects, and spiritualism in particular, believed that he would render a future age valuable service. When this commission started out with the idea of proving the falsity rather than the truth of the subject they plainly demonstrated their own incapacity. Instead of associating themselves with reputable persons, who had given the subject years of attention and thought, they ruled them out as incompetent; and their report is simply a conglomeration of experiences with professional prestidigitators and a few mediums who, for the most part, were foolish enough to attempt any manifestations under the unfavorable conditions furnished. They started out with two or three clumsily constructed supposititious spiritual personalities, and sought to gain communication with them, all the while knowing that no such persons had ever existed; and the report shows that, however great humbuggery there may be in spiritualism, there was not a little hypocrisy and deceit among the professors at the University. Honest they may have been, but intelligent and honorable they were not. Following these, a society for psychical research was formed, which began by ignoring spiritual mediumship altogether, and, after meandering on its way for some time, turned its attention to the study of apparitions in graveyards, and finally ended its career by burying itself therein.

Out of this, indirectly, the psychical society grew, which is largely made up of clever clergymen who, seeing the tendency of the age, wish to prepare themselves so that they will be able to jump in time. In the published book called "Psychical Facts," by the Rev. Minot Savage, this clergyman has carried on his investigations with more or less zest; but he was careful not to endorse his own conclusions and experiences, for fear of being called a spiritualist, before the auspicious moment arrived. We would say to these gentlemen, in all kindness, if your own form of religion be satisfactory and true, why bother with spiritualism, and, if it is not, why not give it up and devote yourselves to something that is. Again, having raised a standard by which the claims of spiritualism should be measured, and having declared that every step taken by you must be proven beyond peradventure, is it wrong for the spiritualists to demand the same proof of the claims that you have been making during the past century, and ask a demonstration as absolute for your statements as you demand for theirs? And shall not the clergyman who cannot give them be deemed as much a deceiver and a fraud as a medium who offers spurious manifestations, claiming them to be genuine? We do not say this in any captious spirit whatever, but only as a matter of self-justification.

Strange to say that, among the investigating clergymen referred to, many are psychics possessing various phases of mediumship in different degrees of development; and the zeal with which they enter into these investigations has been largely created by their previous knowledge of the philosophy of spiritualism, and their high regard for its moral and religious worth. It takes a rogue to fully appreciate an honest man, and this can be well adapted to these psychical investigators, many of whom have been fitted for their high calling in the Spiritualistic Lyceum, or financially enabled to obtain their education by some large-hearted spiritualist. Thus they are in a position, from the start, to judge well of the dearth of truth which is generally found in theology, and the wealth of knowledge contained in the philosophy which, for prudential reasons, they have left behind them.

It takes a philosopher to appreciate a philosophy; and, instead of psychical societies furnishing clergymen to detect fraud, we are led to hope, from our knowledge of the situation, that they are providing well-trained minds, who, knowing the worth of spiritualism, are the better prepared, because of their theological training, to find the real gems hidden in the mine of this gigantic truth.

Spiritualism invites honest enquiry and investigation, but not in the patronizing spirit that has, thus far, influenced societies of this kind, who, if their investigations are successful, would only be recognizing what is already apparent to more than eleven millions of people.

PART XI.

THEOSOPHY AND OCCULTISM.

THEOSOPHY AND OCCULTISM.

(Entered according to Act of Congress, in the year 1893, by AUGUSTA W. FLETCHER, M. D., in the office of the Librarian of Congress at Washington.)

Following in the footsteps of modern Spiritualism, Theosophy and Occultism, together with its much weaker sister, Christian Science, have reared their heads and insist upon a hearing.

The Theosophist declares that he has no connection with the Spiritualists, but has, instead, a resuscitation of ancient religions in modern days. With the majority of the world this assumption has much weight, but, to those who know the alpha and omega of the theosophical movement, it is a trifle amusing. Theosophy which, we are told, defines itself as being God-wisdom—as if all wisdom were not God-like—found its first exponent in Helen Blavatsky and her good-man-friday, Col. Henry Olcott, while sojourning at the Eddy Home, in Chittenden, Vermont, for specific spiritual demonstrations in the form of materialization. The idea of giving to these demonstrations an intelligent bearing suggested itself to these clever people, that is to say, the attendant spirits at the cabinet suggested to them that the time had come when Spiritualism should take its place among the religions of the world. Blavatsky, concerning whose life very little is known, and whose career, from her own stand-point, seemed to have covered more years than are given to most people to live, was familiar with the religions of the East, and also was well read in several different languages. What she lacked in worldly knowledge Col. Olcott, through his newspaper reporting, was able to supply, consequently these two people returned to New York City, called a meeting of influential Spiritualists at the house of a Spiritualist, and then and there started the Theosophical movement. Being unable to govern matters as they wished, and not seeing the possibility for personal notoriety which they desired, these two aforesaid individuals branched off from the society which they had instituted, and were soon launched out upon the sea of speculative thought. Naturally they attracted considerable attention, not from the things that they were able to accomplish, but from the promises they made of future miracles. Then Blavatsky wrote "Isis Unveiled," which book served to envelop "Isis" more completely than all the mysticism of the past had ever done. The volume is interesting, however, from a literary stand-point at least, and some of its chapters are valuable for what they suggest, rather than what they contain. The book shows throughout a most incomplete grasp of the subject, and no purpose whatever, save, perhaps, as a means of venting spite upon all forms of the Christian religion. Then Madam Blavatsky and Col. Olcott sailed away to India, and planted the standard of the movement at Adyar, where the Theosophical temple now is. Then this same Blavatsky began to figure as an independent wonderworker, performing, in a clumsy way, a number of miracles which accomplished little more than to prove that she had but a small possession of occult power;

and yet she was a woman of great magnetic attraction, strength of will, and a personality made of so many peculiarities, that she was bound to attract attention wherever she moved. From India she went to London and various parts of Europe, and Theosophy, having developed in its intellectual scope, began to attract more attention still. Its principal thoughts were the brotherhood of man and the fatherhood of God, and a positive theory of reincarnation. These have always been held by advanced Spiritualists, although, dressed up in new phraseology, they had the appearance of original ideas. But the Theosophist made a strong point against mediumship and insisted that there should be a discontinuance of it, advancing many strange theories in connection with the subject, which are altogether too ephemeral to discuss, but they added a new power which the spiritualists had not before considered, namely, that of adeptship; declaring that instead of persons being controlled by spirits, their efforts should be to control them. And thus Blavatsky, and others, claim that they hold domination over lower disembodied spirits, who infest the atmosphere, and are especially appointed to do their bidding.

This idea renders certain orders of spirits amenable to the hypnotic control of those who are in the body, and who are able to subject these spirits to themselves and, in the accomplishment of any purpose, to use them as so many slaves. Indeed, the entire teaching of Theosophy seems to be in this direction, and whether you begin at the primary step or work your way up alone, it has but the one object in view, namely, of becoming a master, which object is attained only through great self-sacrifice and a development of the powers of the human will.

Many, of course, will start out with the idea that this is easy of accomplishment and, in the early stages of their endeavor, feel most confident of attaining the desired end. But beyond learning a few laws, and trying a number of inconsequential experiments, they fail to transcend the powers of the ordinary mortal. There are others seemingly gifted in this direction who are able to exert an influence which, while its source may be questioned, its presence is undoubted. From the moment such an one enters the room a something is perceptible, and in conversation, manner, and movement this impression is conveyed. That it may be purely hypnotic is possible, and that much that is said to occur in the presence of a master is due to this cause is quite likely, yet the Theosophists insist that the lower spirits pervade the earth, and that the earthly atmosphere and attendant conditions above it can be subjugated by their superior will.

So, when Blavatsky transferred a cigarette from Calcutta, behind a picture in the Louvre, in Paris, she simply took the dainty article from her case, tossed it into the air and one of these invisible adjuncts of her will did the rest. When, at a picnic party, an extra cup and saucer was wanted, and Blavatsky ordered an attendant to dig in the garden, where he found it, it was because one of these invisible beings, having been told by Blavatsky that it would be wanted, had previously buried it, and although, shortly after, Madame and Monsieur Coulomb positively declared that they had been employed to arrange these wonders, they were at once discredited by all true theosophists, although their assertions were established by overwhelming evidence.

It is the aim and object of every theosophist to become an adept, to make himself a positive rather than a negative, and to govern rather than be ruled. Another curious idiosyncrasy of this body is that somewhere in the Himalaya Mountains there is a brotherhood known as the Mahatmas who are, in reality, the governing power of this movement. These extraordinary brothers are said to appear and disappear in different parts of the world at will, but no one has ever seen them, and their existence rests upon the baseless assertion of the Blavatsky satellites, whose only evidence of their existence is the result of the fiction of her wonderfully constructive and imaginative brain. And yet we cannot leave this subject without saying that the *motif* of theosophy is a great and good one; that the intellectual ability of many of its followers has added many contributions to the thought of the day, and that, in a more modified form, it is bound to lead a certain class of minds, at least, to the acceptance of a more universal form of religion. In short, we think it can be justly said that theosophy is the intellectual part of spiritualism, and that spiritualism is the emotional side of Theosophy. This will be readily seen when both the phenomena and philosophy of Spiritualism—imperfectly developed though they may be in their present state—are carefully considered and analyzed.

The teaching of advanced spirits, through their chosen

instruments, are nearly similar to the purpose and object with which theosophy claims to identify itself, while the phenomena that has so marked the present century, is in keeping with anything that the adept has thus far been able to offer; the difference appearing to be only as to the source from which that power springs.

It would seem as foolish for the Theosophist and the Spiritualist to quarrel, as for the Unitarian and the Universalist. All are really journeying on the same road together, with the same point in view, differing only in some minor interpretations, which do not affect the main object of the journey.

That Spiritualism has been largely confined to a demonstration of the phenomena, is due to the fact that human minds, no matter how conclusive the theory may be, require some external evidence before they are able to accept the claims made. The realms of this philosophy have not thus far been traversed extensively by the Spiritualist; he has not theorized to any great extent upon the higher aspects of spiritual law; consequently, the Theosophist in entering into this domain of human interest, finds himself untrammeled in his speculations, and is left free to construct almost any theory that may suggest itself. It will be for the coming century to sift these theories, which we are free to say, in many instances, are far from being authoritative, and separate them as the wheat from the chaff. If he can throw a stronger light upon the phenomena of Spiritualism, and demonstrate that they are produced by any other law than that which is claimed, he will not only render the general public a service, but also every Spiritualist whose object is to gain the truth, no matter at what cost. We find, however, as much divergence of opinion among Theosophists as elsewhere; and the inquirer becomes mystified amidst a whirlwind of conflicting statements, which leave him in doubt as to just what is the ultimate good. This is incidental to the forming of any new system of thought, and will go on until prejudice has eliminated personal animosities, overcome jealousies and created a desire for the highest and best, not only in speaking, but in thinking and living, which shall become the central purposes of every life. Theosophy and Occultism are to Spiritualism what algebra and geometry are to the multiplication table.

So far as Christian Science is concerned, too much cannot be said for its work, especially among religiously inclined people. It has been to such minds invaluable, and, while derided by the church, and laughed at by the public, it has gone on its way accomplishing the the greatest amount of good for a certain class of minds. It teaches that influences of all kinds move in waves, and that, through thought, the individual places himself in relationship with any one of these, which produces an effect according to its nature and kind; good thoughts producing health, and bad thoughts resulting in what is called disease. It insists, however, that all persons may be well and happy if they only put themselves into proper relationship with the great central spirit of all good. The idea of a devil, or a power of evil, is deemed both unchristian and unscientific, there being but one supreme power in the universe. This effort to get at the universal is a valuable one for that class of individuals who have just begun to think, and are not able to stand independent of the church, remembering, always, that children must first be fed upon milk before they are ready for strong food, and, also, that the majority of the world have, as yet, only just been born, mentally. Further on, when the alphabet has been learned, each will begin to think and act for himself, and then the thoughts of others will be valuable only in their suggestiveness.

Are we wrong in saying that modern spiritualism is the tree, and that Theosophy, Occultism and Christian Science are a few of the many branches that grow thereon?

PART XII.

OTHER CONDITIONS IN THE SPIRITUAL LIFE.
THE SUICIDE'S STORY.

OTHER CONDITIONS IN THE SPIRITUAL LIFE.

(Entered according to Act of Congress, in the year 1893, by AUGUSTA W. FLETCHER, M.D., in the office of the Librarian of Congress at Washington.)

It is well, perhaps, in a work of this kind, to refer, although briefly, to those conditions that affect the state of affairs on earth, and which exert an unfavorable influence over those who are in the spiritual world. Passing from this life to the higher life, through the action of a natural law, is one thing; being precipitated into that life by accident or any of the attendant evils of life, looked upon as being outside of nature, is quite another. There being a certain purpose to be out-worked in every human life, whatever interferes with that purpose is bound to produce an effect which will reflect itself unfavorably upon those conditions which follow after. The sudden cutting off of life is bound to react in this way, and those spirits who are hurled into eternity while yet the earth holds strength and positive attractions for them are bound to be held to the sphere of their earthly life until they have withdrawn from it all the requisite magnetic conditions upon which the development of their spirit so much depends. Through the process of disease the magnetic rays, which hold the spirit to the body, are gradually disconnected from it, and when the spirit enters in upon its spiritual estate it finds that the spiritual body has already been built up, and is waiting for its coming. That sickness and pain are the processes of nature through which this object is attained is true, and while death, seemingly, means a great change to the spirit, it, in reality, is no more in its action than the transplanting of a flower from one garden to another. But, even in the case where the patient lingers on the border land for some time, the magnetic conditions are not completed on the instant, and, while the magnetic centre has left a physical body and attracted to itself the stronger elements out of which the spiritual body is built, it still continues to draw from that physical body other requisite elements; and this may extend over a term of years. In fact, so long as the body retains any distinctive relationship to nature, it is bound to exert some influence over the spirit. Thus anything that will interfere with her direct action will produce a result and effect upon the spirit itself. Everything should be left to nature, so far as possible, and in this wise she will furnish a solution of the problem which, without her aid, is bound to be a complicated one.

Cremation, which is coming somewhat to the front in the present day, is, without doubt, the best means of freeing the spirit from all earthly conditions. For it severs the magnetic relationship which has been so long established, and is bound, in spite of everything, to assert itself for a long time. There are very many who have a repugnance to cremation, feeling that burning the body is a most inhuman method. We have observed that those who calmly insist that the souls of sinners must be burned for an eternity pause and hesitate whenever the subject of incineration is introduced.

We do not propose to advance any argument for this process from the stand-point of the living, as to health, etc., although much could be said upon the subject, but rather to deal with the spiritual side of it, and to unqualifiedly state that the moment that the body is reduced to ashes it ceases to attract or affect the spirit in the least degree. It immediately releases all the elements held in bondage to it, and gives it a freedom which, otherwise, it might take years to attain. When this is understood in all its bearings it will be looked upon as a duty to the dead, rather than as a protection to the living.

It is our purpose, however, to speak of a class of spirits who are held to the earth by purely physical conditions, and who are called earth-bound. Wraiths, ghosts and apparitions all belong to this class, and are usually held to some one spot whereon the tragedy of their life was enacted. It is not from choice that they remain in such scenes, not from choice that they appear and disappear at given intervals, but from the action of a law over which they have no control whatever. Such spirits are not recognized as being either advanced or unfolded, or as returning with any definite or distinct purpose; but rather the state of the individual makes it possible for him to apprehend their presence, to recognize their personality, and sometimes, briefly, to hold communion with them. They, for a passage of time, more or less, are attracted to a given place, from whose influence it is impossible for them to escape. The reason for this is apparent when it is understood that the condition by which they were removed cuts off a certain magnetic element pertaining to the body, which the spirit requires, and without which it is impossible for it to pass on its way in a completed form.

A man is murdered and the cord of life which held him to earth is suddenly, and without warning, severed; his blood is spilled on the floor, or on the ground and, in consequence, a part of his physical life is separated from the centre to which it is responsive. The spirit is immediately thrown out of relationship with the elements to which it was formerly connected, and while the major part of the elements required go to build up the spiritual body, there is still much remaining that is disconnected therefrom, and it is an essential that the spirit attract that force unto itself. In fact, it is a necessity that such a purpose be accomplished before the entirety of the spirit is assured, but, through the severing of these elements, the spirit no longer holds a direct attraction over him, and, consequently, is forced to remain as if tied to the spot until, through the passage of time, or the assistance of spirits within or without the body, the magnetic relationships are re-established, and the spirit, in the strength of its full stature, is able to go forth untrammeled. This is the secret, so to speak, of all haunting spirits; and the moans of pain and the sighs and deep groans, which are often heard as emanating from some surroundings, are the same, in nature and quality, as if they had arisen from purely earthly causes. The spirit longs to get away, to break the shackles that bind him, fights against the limitations of his surroundings, as an eagle might against the bars of his cage; but his efforts are unavailing, and he finds himself held in the clutches of a law as inexorable as fate itself; and, passing this term of suffering, he hails the hour of release with great gladness and rejoicing. Kindly disposed and sympathetic mortals who comprehend, at all, the conditions of these spirits are enabled to greatly assist and relieve them, by going to the places where they are thus confined, and, from their own earnest desire, furnish the spirit with those elements of courage and strength whereby he is enabled to more firmly assert his own individuality and claim that which is his own. Mortals placed in such bondage would excite the sympathy of the most apathetic, not only for any physical suffering that might be apprehended, but for the effect upon their spiritual natures. Such spirits, as we have referred to, should enlist the sympathies a thousand times more; and, as expeditions are sent out to ameliorate the conditions of those who are in a plague-stricken district, so also the spiritually-minded can find a sphere of great usefulness in endeavoring to assist those who, through no fault of their own, are placed out of relationship with themselves and the spiritual world.

The suicide furnishes, perhaps, the strongest illustration of this law. A man, finding the burden of life too heavy to be borne, seeks relief in what he foolishly calls the repose and forgetfulness of death. He realizes the sorrows and griefs of the life that are about him, the obligations and duties that he has not the power to fulfill, and would escape them. He, perchance, sees the loss of position, disgrace and dishonor staring him in the face, and may fully comprehend that when to-morrow's sun shall have risen the place will be vacant that he has so long filled, and that his name, heretofore spoken of with respect, has become a by-word in the mouths of those for whose good opinion he cares. Rather than meet these untoward winds of fate, he shuts out the world, forgets the obligations and duties that still remain, and seeks, by one bold stroke, to become master of the situation by taking himself out of it. When the day dawns he has ignored his external obligations, and passed off the stage of active life altogether. Those who would have dealt unkindly are compelled, through the exigencies of the situation, to leave unspoken their bitter thoughts, and deal, as best they can, with the circumstances which, not infrequently, a plain statement of the facts would have wholly cleared up.

But how about that venturesome spirit who has closed the volume of old obligations? Has he found the rest he sought? Has he passed on from the realms of care and duty to a state of rest, wherein he is oblivious to past obligations? Has joy taken the place of sorrow, smiles that of tears, and a complete renovation of nature followed, by which discouragement has been eliminated, and hope, faith and trust given instead? Has he, indeed, left the old world, the old life and the old duties, and begun a new world where fresh motives, nobler impulses and grander possibilities unroll themselves before his wondering vision? Come there no thoughts of the old life, old friends, old duties? No desire to have done battle with fate, and, if defeat had followed at last, to feel that one's best strength had been given in the effort to win the victory? Is there no sense of regret over heavy burdens for others to bear, or home deserted, or faiths broken, or promises unfulfilled? Mistaken, indeed, is he who imagines that release from life, in this way, holds a panacea for the ills of earth. Whatever the outward result may be, it were better to meet it than to endeavor to escape it, for all that death can do is to change one's relationships with life's obligations, but not the weight and the duty that pertains thereto.

The man who, thus rashly, takes the issue of life in his own hands is not able to close the volume by so doing, but is closely held to the earth until the last farthing is paid, the last obligation fulfilled, and the last duty canceled. Centuries may come and go, continents, even, pass away, and his very existence be forgotten, and yet he remain, held to the conditions of a work unperformed, a duty unfulfilled, until the desired effect has been produced upon his spirit, and he has gained that equipoise which is a spiritual necessity. He is compelled to endure not only every pang which would have fallen to his lot, had he lived, but also a twofold punishment which his cowardly treatment of the situation has brought upon him, and as the natural result of his action. And this will seem legitimate enough, and absolutely just, when one takes into consideration that all the experiences and vicissitudes of life come to each individual for the completion of his spiritual nature, and in the line of absolute necessity.

To judge of a life passing through these experiences is to make a mistake common among men, but impossible to advanced spirits. It is only when the result is attained, and the effect upon the spirit apparent, that such judgment is either reasonable or just, and, in every case, the superior wisdom of the all-controlling power that guides and shapes the destinies of man will be evident. The world's greatest success does not necessarily mean that the individual, if this were continued, was receiving that tuition which would best affect him in his development, but as the flowers require light and shade, storm and sunshine, night and day, so every human being requires all the variability of an earthly experience to bring out that which is dormant within him. As the athlete never knows what his strength is until it is tested, so a man is never able to measure himself, spiritually, until he has been called upon to meet the adverse winds of fate, as well as to enjoy the sunshine of prosperity. Indeed, we are bound to say that any man whose force goes out to prosperity alone, develops the worst side of human nature; for those who have enjoyed its results are arrogant, proud, opinionated and unsympathetic. It has been well said, that only the poor can sympathize with the poor; and it might also be added, with equal force, that only those who have tasted the bitter cup of sorrow can understand those who are still called upon to walk through the valley of tears.

No, suffering mortals, whatever your trials, your obligations or your duties, it is better for you now, infinitely better for you through eternity, to meet and bear, as best you can, the scourges of fate, than to aimlessly and foolishly seek to avert them. But if you will not listen, and persist in throwing the burden down when the journey is only half finished, know then that an inexorable law will require of you a fulfillment of every demand, will take the burden up and place it upon your shoulders again, and force you to bear its added weight, until the purpose of life is fulfilled, though it take a century of eternities to accomplish the end; during which time little or no assistance can be rendered you, by mortals or spirits, while in that condition, save, perhaps, by helping you to more readily comprehend your duty and its obligations. The work, you must do for yourselves; and you will find that this very act will separate you from your spirit friends who, having performed their part, are drawn, by the law of attraction, to journey on toward the heights, while you are left behind. Your act will forever stand before you like some menacing spirit, building a barrier between you and the things hoped for; and will, by its presence, continually impress upon your mind that whatever darkness may surround you it is of your own creating, and can only be lifted by your own individual efforts.

Those passing out from this world by accident, will be held, for a time, to the scene of the disaster, it is true; but, since their attitude of mind had nothing to do with the result, they are in a condition to receive any benign influences that advanced spirits may desire to impart, and, consequently, are in a state of temporary disturbance for a time only; just long enough to gain that magnetic equilibrium referred to in the earlier part of this article. But as persons are inspired on the earth by a desire to ameliorate the condition of the unfortunate, and go forth as nurses in hospitals, and angels of mercy to plague stricken households, so there are spirits who hold a mission from high-heaven to minister to those who go to the spiritual world through untoward circumstances; and such spirits are tireless in their efforts to assist those who, thus unfortunately, are hurled into eternity without a moment's warning. Kindly disposed mortals can, through their interest and desire, do much to establish a needed magnetic relationship for the spirit, thereby assisting him to free himself from what would, otherwise, be a most undesirable state.

It will thus be seen that, while the higher spirits are able to labor for the spirits in the flesh, those who are still embodied may be instruments for accomplishing much good for those who have crossed the boundary line of life, but who are yet held amenable to its laws.

The Suicide's Story.

(Entered according to Act of Congress, in the year 1898, by AUGUSTA W. FLETCHER, M. D., in the office of the Librarian of Congress at Washington.)

Life is a hard thing at best. Those who live in the sunshine have not much idea about the chill there is in the shadow. It is easy enough for some; it is hard enough for others; and every man knows his own burden better than he could understand that of another. He is held responsible, by the world, for what he does, for what the world thinks he ought to do, and, failing to do that, he is condemned accordingly. Perhaps those who are the first to judge him would also be the first to commit the offense that they accuse him of.

I am not saying this, God knows, to justify myself in anything that I have done, but just to state how it all appears to me. Looking back over the record of my life, I am sure I tried to do my best, and if I failed more is the pity. That's all. A man cannot be blamed for losing a battle just because his enemy happens to have more strength and better weapons than he; and it is the story of that battle, and the story of the defeat in which it all ended, that I wish to tell you, so that others, who are following in the same path, may, perhaps, gain courage enough to continue to meet whatever the future has in store for them.

My name was Edwin Heatherly and, from my earliest recollections, I have always felt there was no place for me in the world. My father and mother died before I was even old enough to speak their names, and I found a home among their people, who, inspired by duty and family pride, did that which can only be well done when actuated by love. I grew up with them in a home out of which all kindly feeling for me was kept, and with the sense that every mouthful of food that I ate was given in pity.

A loveless childhood is a night without a star, the day without the sun, a world out of which everything has been taken; and yet, I had my thoughts, my dreams and my hopes, that have ever been and will ever be the attendant angels of childhood's hours.

Alone, I used to wander under the grand old trees by the side of the flowing river, looking up to the sky where, in my childish way, I used to think the angels lived; and I wondered if I had an angel-friend who was watching over and guiding my footsteps.

Sensitive and retiring by nature, I found no one in whom I could confide. The people about me, when I tried to talk to them, said I was given to strange fancies; and I was always spoken of as being odd and queer. The instructors and teachers seemed, at first, to understand me somewhat better; but they soon took the impression of those about them, and offered me small sympathy. And so, up to sixteen years of age, in that English home, I found, in the silence of nature, my only comfort.

Having some predilection to art, and inheriting a sum of money through the death of my parents, it was decided that I should go to Genoa, in Italy, to study.

This was my desire, may I not say the realization of my dreams; and, when my uncle and guardian finally consented, it seemed as if there was something within me that was crying out for joy.

I said good-bye, gladly, to the life I was leaving and to the people who were in it, and looked forward to the world in which I was going, with all the enthusiasm born of fulfilled hopes. It seemed to me then, I remember, as if I should surely find that for which my heart was craving; as if I should at last look into eyes that would be able to see the unexpressed within my heart and give me the courage and the understanding of how best to express it. And so I went away from all that I had known, eagerly and earnestly seeking in this new world for the something which my nature demanded, but which circumstances had not given.

In the home of an old artist, just outside the city walls, I found an asylum, so to speak. In him, the fires of youth still burned; and, although he had failed to write his name strongly upon the records of the world, he had found in his artistic work a happiness and a satisfaction which many successful artists know not of. He visited the galleries of the palace where the works of great masters were kept, and which, to this day, are looked upon by the gaping hordes who neither see nor feel an intimation of what true genius is. He taught, also, several others who, like myself, were drinking, early, at the spring of inspiration, and, in a sweet, simple and wonderful way, was able to bring us all into the little world that pervaded his studio, and everything that was in it.

In the early morning, while hill and valley, palace and cot, and the far-reaching waters, were bathed in the rose-light of the awakening day, we would gather unto ourselves something of that spirit of beauty which speaks with greater force to the artistic nature than to the rest of mankind. At eventide, when the day and its work was done, and the mantle of silence rested gently upon the scenes the sun had left, while the stars, ever watchful, held their guard above the sleeping world, fancy would take unto herself new strength, and fly far out over the shining waves, until the sea reached that spot where sky and ocean blend together and the two become one.

Oh! bright and golden were those hours in the old studio, where the master still worked, hoping to realize in the young lives he was training the achievement of that of which he had dreamed, as they were dreaming, but which had never crowned his efforts. He taught us (or rather made us feel) the spirit in art, —the spirit that abides in everything—and whatever the nature of our work, whether it was historical or personal, we were made to look behind all evidences of life, for that which was life itself. And so the years wore on, and that, which had been but a bud, unfolded itself into an open flower; and I began to feel that all the loss which had marked my earlier youth was more than repaid in the work which heaven had made it possible for me to do.

I could never express myself in words as some can, but when I stood before the easel with palette and brush in hand, the canvas and the color would voice the thoughts within my soul. I seemed to be in another world or, if in this world, to be permitted to look upon another, where I met people, witnessed scenes, and enacted parts which bore no relation to my other life. Sometimes, the good old master would say, "you should have been a poet instead of an artist; you are a poet and an artist in one." And then he would say to me, "you will some day do what I hoped to do. I see myself leaving this world and giving you my life to complete as I would have done had I the power." And the old man's face would lighten up with such a gentle smile that it would become almost beautiful to look upon.

I had reached my twenty-fifth year, with everything before me bright and encouraging. My art was my consolation, my work was my comforter. I met, at this time, two persons, of whom I shall speak; for upon my connection with them the destiny of my life turned, and subsequent events were dependent.

One, whose name, even now, I must speak with reverence and affection, was a woman of nearly my own age, who was following the same path in which I was working, and whom I met often in the galleries, when studying some of the celebrated masters, whose works still rise, as monuments, to the greatness of their genius. We met, and, from the first moment we looked into each other's eyes, we loved. It was the old, old story, told in many lands, repeated in many tongues. The other was a young gentleman of title and position, a Spaniard by birth, who was playing with art as many do who are weary of the attractions of the world. He was making life a long, reckless holiday, and often stung the flower from which he had extracted the honey. I knew him, for he had been to our studio for a short time. He saw the woman whom I, with all my artistic nature, had idealized into an angel, and, falling under the gentle sway of her influence, desired to accomplish his own ignoble ends, at whatsoever the cost might be. We were all three thrown together, more or less; we were all three working upon what was to be our masterpiece, which, when the day arrived, was to be hung in the academy and, perhaps, win the appreciation of those who passed it in review.

I cannot tell you what it means to one who has worked for years, and feels within himself all the force of a great inspiration, when the opportunity for its realization is at hand.

I had everything to labor for: love, art and myself. And so the work progressed, and so love grew between Alixe and myself, and a friendship, which I cannot understand, even to this day, between the Spanish gentleman and myself. He was all kindness to me, and all devotion to my sweetheart, and seemed ever to be present in our midst.

My work was finished, and we three were all standing in the old studio together. Alixe was looking at the work I had wrought, which was the death of Juliet; and the face was that of the woman I loved. My thoughts were more upon whether the picture would be accepted or not, than upon anything else; and I bade them both good night at the door, and watched them walk down the pathway, cityward, together. I gave one long farewell look to the dear Romeo and to the dying Juliet, in whose staring eyes, already the light of a better world was shining. Then I went to my room and to sleep. How long I slept I cannot say; but a noise disturbing me, I awoke, and hurriedly, my mind intent upon my picture, went below to see if all was well with it.

There it stood, in the moonlight, by the window, slashed across with two ugly sword-cuts that completely ruined it, and, as I cried out in the agony of despair, "Who has done this thing!" the shadow of a man passed out through the half-opened casement. All the night, with eyes wet with tears, I knelt before my crushed idol; but the face of my love was ever in my heart, and, I thought, when the morning should come, I could, at least, get some consolation from her.

Day broke, the sun rose, and, weak and trembling, I sought her resting-place; but, ere I had reached the house, a youth half-passed, turned and spoke to me, at the same time handing me a bunch of early Spring blossoms, from the heart of which I took a delicately folded note and, on reading it, learned that the wealth and position of her Spanish friend meant to her more than the love of an artist whose world was yet all before him.

I cannot tell you how it was, I only know that my brain seemed on fire; the work of all the best years of my life was ruined, utterly destroyed; the one human being whom I ever truly loved had turned her face toward another, and I, half frenzied, stood alone. It seemed to me as if there was nothing in the world to live for; the despair in my heart was so great that I could not even feel anger at the treachery of mine enemy who had, by one foul blow, destroyed the dream of my life, and taken from me what would have given to existence its highest joy.

Foolish! foolish! foolish! you will say it was, and like a rash youth who, untrained in methods and thoughts, had worked and loved until heart and brain had become frenzied with the fire of ambition. All I know is, I could neither think nor reason; I could not face my old master who had watched every touch of the brush, and who felt that my work was his work. I could not face my fellows and say to them that the one being in whom faith and trust had found their abiding-places had sold herself, and, thereby, placed her foot upon an honest love.

So, without returning to the house, without looking into the face of a human being whom I knew, without saying a word of farewell to my old master and faithful friend, I rushed on, wildly, leaving the noise of the awakening dawn behind me, until I reached the cliffs that overhung the waters of the lower bay. Knowing not, caring not, thinking not, I paused for a moment to take a long farewell look upon scenes endeared by sweet and holy associations, and then hurled myself, with all the strength of which I was possessed, into the waters beneath me.

I remember nothing more to this day of that circumstance. I recall only the icy chill that seemed to freeze me through and through. A sense of escape from somebody and something, anywhere, everywhere beyond the power of individual thought, and from out that mad delirium, I awoke to find myself in another world, and yet so within this, that, while I could see and hear everything, I could neither be seen nor heard myself.

In the little chapel, by the hillside, my body lay; a few friends were there; a kindly priest was saying the last words, and my old master, bowed with years and shaking with grief, was kissing me farewell. Then the scene changed and I, who had sought to escape life and all the responsibilities that it brought, was in the very vortex of life itself, moved by all its emotions, filled with all of its desires, seeing the same people, visiting the same scenes, watching the same work as before, and yet, my heart filled with a nameless horror, was unable to change a single circumstance or influence a single event.

If I had felt in earlier days that I was alone, that there was no place for me, how much more did I feel abandoned and out of place in this unreal world, to which, by so rash an act, I had brought myself. I felt like unto one who longs to speak, but is dumb; who longs to hear, but is deaf to every sound; who longs to see, and yet is blind.

Time passed on, and, one by one, those whom I knew went on their several ways in the world, played their part, and then came hitherward. Each, in looking upon me, saw what I had done; and to all the inhabitants that felt my surroundings, it was known as to who and what I was.

It seemed as if all that I had passed through was written upon my face in letters of living fire, which everyone could read as they passed me by. There was a sense of watching for something that never came, a seeking for something that could never be found, a wandering through the old haunts, looking upon old scenes, watching changes as they came into the lives of old friends, and yet, having no part in it, seeing light, yet being in darkness, looking upon the feast, and yet fainting through hunger and thirst.

Time, like the current of a mighty river that it is, swept on its way, and gradually, through associations with others who were congenial to it, my spirit-self began to feel that there was some hope of release by and by.

Like a prisoner bound in a dungeon, under the earth, who counts the passing days and nights until he sees, in the distance, like a beacon light, the day that shall bring deliverance, so I, after long watching, beheld a spirit whose gentle heart was moved to pity by my intense anguish, and who showed me how, by determined effort, I could conquer and overcome myself. It was not an easy thing I had to do; not a step I had to take, which would, at once, lead me in pleasant paths, but, instead, every inch of the way had to be fought, the bitter dregs of experience had to be drunk, until the elements of wounded vanity and selfish disappointment had been removed from my spiritual nature.

My mother, whom I had not known as a child, was my angel-teacher; from her words, in another way, I learned the lessons of the higher life, which, had they been imparted, in childhood's days, by the same gentle voice, the dark tragedy of my life would have been averted.

I saw, as she pointed downward, that my feet were

deeply buried in the mire of the earth's conception; selfishness, pride and wounded vanity had been the wicked spirits who had pushed me over the cliff, and I still remained amenable to their malign influences. They were torn out as weeds are uprooted in the garden, and, one day, I found myself freed from all these earthly things.

In that moment I knew what life was; I seemed to stand above and not with it, and could easily recognize all of those emotions which sway the human mind. Behind me lay the past, shrouded with a darkness indescribable, before me the future stretched like a silver line leading to those realms elysian, where happy spirits dwell. The music of their voices I could faintly catch, and the beauty of their sphere I could dimly see; but it was not for me; I could not hope to attain unto it until a still greater change was wrought within myself.

In place of the old, vindictive thoughts, a kindly forgetfulness had come; and the very day that I began to realize what there was beyond me, I stood, face to face, with the woman and the man upon whose actions my destiny had turned.

They, too, in their earthly life, after the first wild intoxication was over, had found its sorrows and miseries. The law of compensation had shadowed their lives, and they stood, now, in the spiritual world, asking help from me whom they both had so wickedly betrayed; and, seeing them in sore distress, my only thought was to extend to them the helping hand of a brother and a friend.

In that moment my own redemption was assured; I

had shown, by that act, that I, at least, was ready for the better life, and, from that time and throughout all future years, my spirit will be enabled to seek its own, to carry on, in a better way, the studies that had so interested me when here in the earth life.

Think of me, if at all, as one who, passing through great suffering, has risen above it, and is now freed from its influence.

Despairing mortals, whoever and wherever you may be, think not that to you is given the power of changing the decrees of fate. Think not that one of life's duties can be left undone; that there is an escape from that inexorable law upon the fulfillment of which everything depends. Bear your burdens as best you can, walk through the valley of tears with a strong heart, live to yourselves and to your duties as you understand them, and know that however great the suffering and disappointment may be, through apparent failures of earth, they are less in magnitude than are those that come through placing yourselves out of relationship with the duties that must be performed.

The hope that many have of escape, means a changing of conditions, it is true; but the old duties, the old requirements are bound to follow you whithersoever you may go. Take ye, then, the words of one who knows, full well, whereof he speaks. Life, in whatever condition it naturally asserts itself, cannot be improved upon; and whatever the rash hand of man may do to change its direction, will but result in adding to its burdens, in increasing its sorrows and impeding the development and growth of the individual spirit itself.

PART XIII.

A GLIMPSE INTO THE SPIRITUAL WORLD.

A Glimpse into the Spiritual World.

(Entered according to Act of Congress, in the year 1893, by AUGUSTA W. FLETCHER, M. D.,
in the office of the Librarian of Congress at Washington.)

That the world, and the life beyond this, should seem to be unnatural and unreal, is to be expected, from the stolid state that the human mind has been in, during the development of financial and commercial interests, wherein the highest purpose of life has been to gain earthly advancement, and to control all human desires and emotions, so that they should bend, exclusively, to this end. Intimations of the higher life are accordingly lost amidst the jargon of selfish interests, as strains of sweetest music are unrecognized amidst the noise and contention which drowns them. In the earlier age of the world these interests had not been developed to any great degree, and the consequence was that men of poetical and contemplative tendencies were able to place themselves in close relationship with nature, and receive, directly, from her hand, such gifts of inspiration as would serve to ennoble and upbuild. The requirements were less in those days; men fought less for position, and were better satisfied with the returns that life brought than now. The fever of unrest, so contagious in active communities, had not yet developed itself; and the blue sky, the shining waters, the mountains and valleys all held a suggestiveness of peace which, to-day, is passed by unseen and unrecognized. No wonder, then, that much that is best in art, poetry and philosophy was apprehended by minds seeking for the highest, and still continues to hold itself as a standard for competitive comparison with the very strongest efforts of the present age. It is not that any realm of truth has been lost, any kingdom of the mind destroyed, or world of thought obliterated, that we receive, to-day, so little that is lasting and valuable; but it is because the mind sustains a different relationship to opinions and thoughts, and seeks to interpret the laws and forces of nature from an entirely different stand-point.

The great ocean of truth washes the shores of eternity with as mighty waves of thought, to-day, as in the centuries that have gone, when Socrates walked along the sands, and Plato and Pericles sent their wise spirits far out over its wastes, and brought back the shining pearls of thought which remain, undimmed, through the passage of time, and are still held as among the richest treasures in the casket of the world. But, in the present time, the laws of nature are resolved down to their practical bearings, and the commercial side of truth is emphasized, while the more sentimental, or, if you please, human, is quite overlooked. Yet, all the while, there come moments to every life, no matter how perplexed and burdened it may be, when it seeks to penetrate these earthly clouds, and pass beyond the temporary limitations that mark the boundary line of a lifetime. All dream of a condition when the soul shall be at peace with itself and its surroundings, of a state of life where buying and selling, profit and loss, victory and defeat, shall play no part whatever, where all the interests of humanity shall merge themselves into one universal law, and all things, now so divergent in their character, shall be brought together in sweet accord. Utopian the thought, without doubt, and yet, when you look back over the pathway of the past and see how the influences of the earth, from warring with each other, have become amicably associated in nearly all their relations, where the interests of one became, through this interblending, an interest of equal importance to the other, it is not impossible to conceive of a state wherein all human interests are mutual and all benefits common. What is one's loss is said to be another's gain; but that relates to material things only. The spiritual interpretation of this statement is that no one can gain through the loss of another; that where one loses, if such a thing were possible, all lose; and where one gains all are likewise benefited. And thus, from out of all this highest conception, man builds up the hereafter, eliminating all elements of discord, while adding to it all those blessed dreams which were too beautiful and grand for any earthly realization. Thoughts are but buds on life's tree, needing the changing atmosphere of varied experiences before they bloom in the lands beyond the valley of death.

The spiritual world lies around this world, and sustains the closest possible relationship to it. It is divided into spheres and states, according to the development of its inhabitants, just the same as this world is divided by like mental and social positions. It might be likened to a flight of stairs with the lower step resting upon the earth, where all of those spirits dwell whose thoughts and interests turn continually earthward. On the next step will be found those in whose nature spiritual and material things are blended with equal force, and the next where the aspirations are spiritward, with still the reflection of earthly interest upon them; and so on, until, upon the highest step, the spirit has divested itself of everything which could impede its advancement, and is prepared to enter into a state of complete repose, or take up the earth-life again under entirely different aspects and conditions.

It must not be imagined that spirits are separated from each other by either walls or conditions that are impenetrable, any more than are the different classes of minds on earth. To be sure, in the earth sphere, society is compelled to protect itself from some of its members who would trespass on the rights of others, and these are held in certain forms of bondage, and justly so, we should say; but the rest of the world is permitted to move at will, governed by whatever impulses it may be inspired, within the certain limitations that civilization has laid down; and a single city will contain the depths and the heights of human life. Depravity as dark as night, and generosity as free as the sun, may walk along, side by side, and be almost oblivious one of the other. It is not places or distance that marks the distinction, it is the individual state, which, from the various relationship of things, is compelled to manifest an entirely different result. The highest man can descend to the lowest depths, and yet be able to return to his own sphere again; but the lowest can never rise beyond his natural condition until he has disconnected himself from those elements that hold him down. This law always governs the condition of every spirit in the spiritual world.

On the lower step, we find a class of spirits who are called the Dwellers on the Threshold, who, although in the spiritual world, have no impulse toward it, but are as material, vindictive and selfish in their desires as before they passed through the narrow portals of death. They have simply dropped the outer covering of the body, retaining all of its passions and animosities; and, like so many hungry wolves, are seeking to satisfy their thirst and hunger, upon any element that may present itself. These spirits are held, by the law of earthly attraction, to the scenes they have just left, and are best pleased when they can associate themselves with a nature equally as depraved as their own, and, thereby, repeat and re-repeat the destroying passions of their earthly lives. Every drunkard, every thief, every murderer has attendant spirits of like character, who find their highest enjoyment in re-enacting the old scenes of their life. They give to the human mind greater cunning and greater power of invention, to the arm, greater strength, and to the individual, himself, greater indifference to whatever penalties may be attached to his wrong-doing. And it is not until such spirits have received an interior awakening, which is bound in time to come, that they see the folly of their ways and the wickedness of their lives. This sphere is called the Sphere of Transition, and in and through it all the conditions, impulses and purposes of the earth are found. Whatever exists on earth finds a spiritual representation there; and the conditions of that sphere are as actual and real, to those who dwell therein, as are houses and lands to those of the earth. The employments and occupations are not dissimilar; but the results obtained are, by far, less satisfying, thus suggesting to the more thoughtful, at least, something beyond. In fact, many of these occupants do not know, for a long time, that they have passed through the change called death, but feel as if they were still passing through some wild dream from which they would shortly awaken. This is commonly true of persons who have been trained in severe schools of theological thought, who are not infrequently drawn to the church wherein they were accustomed to worship, and where they persistently remain, expecting to be transported to the realms of light; and when told, as they often are, that such a journey must be made by and through their own individual efforts, they refuse to listen or believe, saying, to the high angel-teachers who are endeavoring to instruct them in the right way: "You are all deceivers sent to mislead the very elect; we will not believe you; depart, for the Lord will soon be here!"

And then they fall back into that state of mental assurance, which is closely allied to lethargy, to await an event which will never occur. These spirits are the most difficult of all to instruct or lead; for such is their egotism that they are unwilling to believe what is told them, holding that the more logical the statements the more likely they are to be of evil origin; just as some of the theologians on earth declare that the demonstrations of natural science are but the means that his satanic majesty is using to lead astray the souls of the righteous. After a time, probably a very long time, the light of truth illumines even these ignorant natures, and they, through a process of spiritual unfoldment, rise to higher estates. But such a man as John Calvin or Cotton Mather would be in the spiritual world a century, and be followed by hordes of devotees, before a single ray of light could penetrate the density of their natures.

From the Sphere of Transition, the earth planet seems like a world of darkness, over which different human interests hang, like so many clouds, oftentimes nearly obscuring the view. Here and there upon the earth a bright light will appear which, if followed out, will reveal an individual, or a part of the community, inspired by more ennobling purposes than are the rest of their fellows. Over each locality will be found the spiritual world that pertains thereto; or, in other words, over China the invisible influences of the atmosphere are more harmonious to the inhabitants of that part of the country, which locality furnishes a magnetism in which spirits pertaining to it are most at ease. This Sphere of Transition, through which every spirit must pass, extends as far as the atmosphere of the earth. No spirit can be said to be actually in the spiritual world, governed by its laws, and inspired by its higher purposes, until this Sphere of Transition is past. Roman Catholics recognize its existence in a dim way, and hold that even their most devout adherents must pass through it on their way toward the realms of bliss;

and, in order to facilitate the passage, a candle is placed in the hand of the dead, to light him on his way. If, by the burning of one candle, such a journey can be accomplished, it were easily done, indeed; but there are very few who would be able to start, even if the requisite tapers were at hand.

From what we have said, then, be it understood that the first sphere of the spiritual world contains, in essence, everything that exists in external life. It is the mighty laboratory of which all that you see, and hear, and feel, is but the result; that those who enter its border-lands carry with them earthly feelings and sensations, motives, and desires which, with great perversity, they still continue to outwork; and it is only after experience has demonstrated the inefficiency of the aforesaid, that the spirit breaks the shackles it brought from the earth, and, like a bird once pinioned and now set free, lifts itself upon the wings of a noble aspiration, and, thereby, enters upon a career, the ultimate of which is known only to God himself. Having then divested himself of the conditions of the earth, conquered his prejudices, overcome his selfishness, and forgotten, in part, at least, his personal desires and enjoyments, and being aware that all of these must be merged into the law of common good, the spirit enters in upon his work in the spiritual realms, which are removed from the reflex action of the earth, and opens up possibilities heretofore unknown. And, for the first time, such a spirit begins to enter in upon the realization of his own capacities. Not the capacities of the body, for that has been left behind, nor yet the mind, for in the spiritual world that plays a secondary part; but to those possibilities of the spirit which use both the mind and the body to manifest their attributes, and yet transcend them in their most perfect fulfillment. The spiritual body has become changed into the likeness of the spirit, and the affections have either become modified or extended to that degree whereby they enable the spirit to use them without interference.

This first state of the spiritual world we should call the Sphere of Unselfishness; for in it spirits labor for the benefit of the many, regardless of any direct effect upon themselves. It is a sphere of service wherein all who labor in the vineyard are desirous of doing whatever is possible to ameliorate the condition of those who are struggling against the temptations below them, at the same time unfolding whatever possibilities there may be within themselves. It is, perhaps, only just to say, that this is the process of unfoldment; as no spirit in the body, or out, ever speaks a kind word, or proffers kindly assistance, without receiving in return for it (be it unselfishly done) a greater benefit than he confers. This sphere is in direct connection with the earth, by lines of magnetic light, which penetrate the atmosphere of the Sphere of Transition and the physical air as well, and are attached to countries, communities, associations and individuals, who are in affiliation with it. These they are able to supply with a great magnetic force which, ultimately, conquers all obstacles, breaks down barriers, and carries forward the civilization of the world. In this sphere, art, music, literature and every phase of reform exists, in a more perfect state, and it is from this centre that those engaged in like work on the earth derive their highest inspirations. If there be an age when the arts and sciences thrive more at one time than another, it is because a certain number of minds are responsive to this sphere in the spiritual world.

Such men, be they on the platform, in the studio, or wielding the pen, become as prophets to the age in which they live. Mozart, Mendelssohn and Beethoven were men of great musical capacity; but no student of their works can fail to recognize how uneven in quality their compositions are. These men were, by organization and life, susceptible to the inspirations of a higher sphere of the same kind, in the spiritual world, and, without doubt, their compositions were as much a marvel to them as to the world at large. For, in the realm of genius, there is no absolute standard. Surroundings, conditions and temperaments form the degrees of inspiration, and let there be any interference with one of these and the result is immediately circumscribed. Could you have seen the spiritual surroundings of these musicians you would have found that they were closely allied to men of like temperaments in the spiritual world; and the "Song Without Words" of Mendelssohn, and the "Sonatas" of Beethoven, while so little understood or admired by the many, reveal the laws of a divine harmony to the few, indicative of what is one day to be expected generally. Wagner wrote, not to the standard of his generation, but to the standard of his spiritual conception, and his works, when first produced, were honored by being called "the music of the future." But he worked on, all the same, receiving an impulse to continue from the very denunciation visited upon him; and, to-day, the sublime melodies which contain no music for the many are suggestive and almost divine to those who are unfolded in this direction. Thus progress, or growth, ever has been and ever will be but a reflection, on earth, of the higher attainments in the spiritual world.

Raphael painted, with matchless skill, such forms of divine beauty that they stand out, to-day, as revelations of a possible motherhood, and the church has adopted many of them to more fully illustrate its teachings. His works were not simply confined to color, graceful outline, or skillful combination, but all this they were, with an individualized spirit put into them, through which some divine sentiment speaks to every beholder, in language so potent that even the most obtuse realize its influence. Raphael was the medium for the Sphere of Art, and while all honor and praise are due to him as a worker, none the less, without the inspiration above and beyond him, that work would never have been accomplished.

Perhaps, after all, the reformer evidences more of the power of the spirit than almost any other. That is, the power is more appreciable from the human side, for, without apparent reason, he throws everything in the scale: earthly prospects, earthly ambitions, oftentimes the respect of the community and his position in society, and embarks upon a sea of troubles, steering for some unknown harbor and never satisfied until he has discovered such an one. It could not be supposed that

Jesus of Nazareth, from choice, took up the cross which liberal thought ever imposes upon its votaries, lived a life of suffering, and endured a death of ignominy, from any other than a disinterested motive; that Joan of Arc left her quiet home, on the hillside, to engage in all the horrors of warfare, save at the call of some intelligence superior to herself, or that the founders of this country would have risked the dangers of an unknown sea for simply personal results. Or, again, in later days, that Wendell Phillips and William Lloyd Garrison started out on lines of reform which, from the very moment of their inception, meant social ostracism to them; and what they were to the negroes, Theodore Parker, with his grand utterances, was to the world of slaves whom theology has held in a thralldom scarcely less ignominious than that which bound the slaves of the South.

All of these men, and ten thousand others whom we might name, were responsive to a corresponding sphere in the spiritual world. Who shall say that he who holds the destiny of mankind in his hand did not see that they would be needed, and sent them into the world to accomplish, for its inhabitants, a result that could be outworked in no other way? True it is they gave forth no uncertain sound; they were superior to all the anathemas hurled against them, and, from the sublime heights of eternity, look down upon the world, feeling that their sufferings were as naught in comparison with the great result gained for humanity. Nor would this idea discount, at all, the usefulness of the individual, or take from him one whit of the honor due his noble efforts; for with him lies, more than with any one else, the forming of those conditions wherein fruition is possible. Sacrifices without number, disappointments unrecorded, and a sadness almost overwhelming, have, at times, fallen with prostrating power upon his spirit.

"I have a strength the world knows not of," said Jesus. It was the strength of the spirit perpetual and eternal, flowing in upon the individual life, that made the suggestion of failure impossible, and overcame all opposition, and which swept away, with one masterly stroke of its hand, all of those contending conditions which a non-appreciative and a non-comprehensive age have forever built up between the reformer and the purposes he desired to accomplish. This was, and is, a spiritual strength derived from spheres above the earth, which float in upon the reformer in the still hours of the night, helping him first to strengthen himself, and then giving him the impulse to go forth to strengthen others in the great battle of right against wrong. The inspiration of these men, and of many others, is accepted by the world, to-day, mistaken and impracticable though they often call it; but the source of the inspiration is not recognized, and it remains for the spiritual teacher to designate the sphere from which it is derived.

Be it herein said, then, that every man with a strong purpose allies himself to a sphere in the spiritual world wherefrom strength for its accomplishment can be obtained, that no human being goes forth single handed and alone, that, however many earthly friends he may have, there is a larger number of spiritual attendants who are in sympathy with him. There are more for him than against him; but they are not the men of earth, for they, at best, are only followers in the footsteps, and are seldom, if ever, little more than a burden for the reformer to carry.

When these men, who have played so important a part in the affairs of the world, are translated, they, after conquering all peculiar personalities, enter into the same sphere from which they received their inspiration while on earth. They at once take up that work which, to them, was so valuable and important. It must, however, be remembered that, no matter how grand the inspiration, it is dependent upon the earthly organization for its expression. Thus, Jesus, while teaching the broadest charity, overturned the tables of the money changers in the temple, cursed the fig tree, and cried out in despair, in the supreme moment: "My God, why hast thou forsaken me!" Other reformers, for the moment, have lent an ear to the flattering tongues of the world, and forgotten the sanctity of their mission and purpose; this is simply the human side, and, by the law of contrast, only serves to emphasize the spiritual expression the more.

The spiritual world is a world of principles to which are attracted all those who are in sympathy with them; and, instead of being a land of forgetfulness or heavenly bliss, the highest joy that a spirit knows is through blessing and benefiting others. The affairs of earth are of every interest to those occupying positions in the spiritual world; and, not infrequently, some one who has attained an altitude unknown upon earth willingly leaves his centre of work in spirit life, steps down to earth, assumes human form, and becomes, while so doing, the embodiment of high spiritual laws. Misunderstood and reviled he will be; pursued and persecuted he will pass from one town to another, and when, at last, the age will find a culmination of its wrath in executing him, he will be able to turn his eyes to heaven, asking God to forgive his enemies, saying, "they know not what they do;" and, having endured every human insult and physical pain, he passes quietly into the spiritual world, not having heard or felt one of the shafts that have been hurled against him. Such men have been condemned in their own age, yes; but emulated through succeeding ones; yet they, in spirit, were quite oblivious to the blame or the praise that human lips could utter.

We have endeavored to show you the conditions of life in the higher states of the spiritual world; but it is manifestly impossible, in the limited use of words extant, and the more limited possession of ideas, to dwell upon those states which have no corresponding value in the earth. It would simply be dealing in what would appear to be insignificant generalities, and would convey no meaning whatever to the human mind. Those states await the coming of the unfolded spirit, and have no direct bearing upon those laws controlling human life.

Be it known that the lowest spheres of the spiritual world, however superior to the earth they may be, are more or less subjected to the influence and guidance of those spirits who dwell above them, and who are as much more powerful and intelligent than they as is the highest condition of earth above the lowest. Sometimes, it is true, these spirits are instrumental in inaugurating important movements, both on the spiritual and earthly plane; but they move without direct personality, and work wholly indifferent to any appreciable recognition; seeking to hide their identity in their work, and declaring that names are nothing, and attributes everything. Such spirits are above even the Sphere of Unselfishness. Occasionally, they may influence, directly, mediums on the earth plane; but usually their work is purely in the spiritual spheres, or, if they are brought in connection with the earth at all, one or more lesser spirits are used as intermediaries. Thus, the personal control of a medium can only be a step higher than the medium himself; but that same control may derive its intelligence from the highest spheres known in the spiritual world. But such a communication must ever be subject to the keenest examination of the one who receives it; and if it is not capable of bearing such investigation it probably is not from the source that it claims to be. Every high spirit will demand that you use your very best judgment and fullest discrimination, and accept only that which will stand the test.

We hereby refer, in the following, to those more interesting demonstrations which partake of direct personal characteristics; in other words, the communications received from departed friends would appear to have no connection with what we have previously said, and it behooves us, therefore, to devote our attention, for a time, to the consideration of such communications.

Spirits who return to the earth for the purpose of holding communication with their friends are those in whose nature earthly remembrances and associations still play a prominent part. They are, for the most part, attracted to the sphere of their former earthly activities, and usually, in communicating, are held to them. The welfare of an earthly friend is to them of importance; they will joy in his joy and sorrow in his sorrow, and manifest those traits which were the all-governing force of their lives. When asked about the spiritual world, they will always reply in a vague manner; for, in reality, beyond being in a state of general contentment and satisfaction, they know little or nothing of it. Thus the man of business follows its cares as a spirit, the mother watches over her children, and the friend follows the footsteps of his friend, seemingly wholly engrossed in whatever is of earthly interest, and looking forward to the time of the culmination of earthly hopes and for that reunion which is sure to come later on. It must be remembered that much, if not all of the trouble that arises on earth, grows out of the misunderstanding of individuals and motives, rather than through the spirit of contention. Thus a spirit, being able to perceive these motives and purposes, discriminates between what appears to be and what really is, and mistakes are, accordingly, avoided. The mask of deceit is torn from the face of the hypocrite, and pretenses are blown away like chaff before the wind. The assumption of good feeling and kindly content for selfish purposes, which, oftentimes, passes in the world as genuine friendship, is easily penetrated by the clear eye of the spirit. People who on earth pass years side by side with each other, acting a lie and pretending to be what they are not, stand forth in their true guise in the spiritual world, and they are known by all who come in contact with them as having played the part of the deceiver and hypocrite. Brothers and sisters, husbands and wives, parents and children who are held together by no stronger tie than that of blood, will find that death simply relegates and gives to each relation its proper position.

Communicating spirits, then, use mediums as a means of expressing their thoughts; and about the same amount of credence and acceptation should be given to their words as if uttered by the same persons on earth. It is, however, a matter of great pleasure for spirits to thus express their thoughts, and does not hold them back from the path of progress, as some teachers aver. The son who, loving his mother, feels that she is with him on all occasions hesitates before he enters the path of vice; the man who feels that all is lost because some loved one lies beneath the sod gathers much consolation from the whispered words of that loved one as she comes to him, from her spirit home; and all who walk in the pathway of this world, shadowed by sorrow and grieved by despair, gather consolation and strength from the assurances constantly being received that there is no death. We live beyond the grave, and one day, when life's sad drama shall have ended, we will take up, in fairer realms, the broken threads of our lives and be happy again.

PART XIV.

SOME OF THE SUBTLE LAWS OF LIFE.

SOME OF THE SUBLTLE LAWS OF LIFE.

(Entered according to Act of Congress, in the year 1893, by AUGUSTA W. FLETCHER, M. D.,
in the office of the Librarian of Congress at Washington.)

There are very few students who have devoted either strength or time to the study of that interior cause, the outworking of which, in all its varied shades of meaning, makes up the sum of human joys and sorrows. The impulses that are daily manifested in our contact with the world, and the individuals we meet, are but little understood as to their nature or purpose; and the results accruing from their exercise may be a subject of regret and dissatisfaction.

That there is an emotional nature, behind which the *ego* stands, endeavoring to realize its desires, is true; but just what the manifestation of this nature should legitimately be, and what the purpose of such demonstration of emotion may mean is, for the most part, a matter of conjecture and surprise. Within certain limits, these evidences, whatever they may be, are accepted as being natural and right, since they are within the range of the majority of experiences from which the standard of naturalness has been built. Any expression that transcends these limits is looked upon as unnatural; and, if of a pronounced character, becomes a subject for the condemnation of society. But who is there in this age that is able, with all the wisdom that the world contains, to define what morality really is, to measure the heights and the depths of all possibilities, and to rear barriers which shall separate the one to be accepted from the one to be rejected? Surely there is no stamping ground which man's nature has not; for whatever exists in life is a part and parcel of it. What seems to be unnatural, and resulting in abnormality, is not, infrequently, due to the attitude that we sustain toward that nature, and to our limited and circumscribed means of interpreting its laws.

Temperaments, organizations and constitutions are formed, in the first instance, not by the desire of the individual, but are handed to him ready made. The higher mind often repudiates and decries the desires of the body, which, in spite of all internal reasoning, will assert and manifest themselves. How far society has the right to assume a censorship in this matter has been, is, and doubtless will continue to be, a subject for debate. Society is bound to secure itself against molestation and trespass, and yet, at the same time, to be governed by that sense of high regard for the individual which shall, while it seeks to control him, serve, also, to unfold a higher state within his own organization.

Friendships, alliances and marriages are the result of something more than mere desire; there is an undercurrent at work which brings individuals together and holds them, no matter how temporarily, subservient to a law superior to themselves. The mistake, however, that is made on the part of the individual arises from his interpretation of what temporary conditions may mean, he imagining that ties which then exist are intended to endure throughout eternity. In reality, they have for their intention the outworking of some result which, when accomplished, generally ends in the dissolution of the affinity which was supposed to exist between them. Thus families, friends and communities may sustain the most harmonious relationship to each other, may walk on together in the most perfect accord, and yet, after awhile, without the desire of either, they will change and then begin to drift apart. As soon as this is realized, both make an effort to emphasize the old relationship and feeling, and, for a limited period, this will seemingly be done; but, despite the effort, the fire has burned out, and no matter what is said by one to the other, a distinct change has come. There may be external reasons why this change will be outwardly unrecognized; social position, worldly interests, and the duty that is owed to others, often hold together crumbling alliances, out of which every element of fidelity to that alliance has gone.

In many instances, a man and woman who have lived harmoniously at first, as husband and wife, and finding, through these experiences, their unfitness for that relationship, seem to conclude, without further thought, that they are necessarily unfitted to sustain together *any* harmonious relationship; when, in fact, the worst husband and wife might become the best and truest of friends. The old picture of the cat and dog who, when tied together, can find absolutely nothing to do but snarl and scratch, fitly represents the conditions which are brought about, not so much by the nature of the cat and dog, as the relative positions in which they find themselves. Untie them, put the dog in a sunny corner of the garden, and let him lie down to his afternoon nap with a full stomach, and half a dozen cats may gambol about him without even attracting his attention; and finally one of them, at least, can cuddle up in happy contentment beside him. Take this illustration into the every-day life of men and women, and you will find it *a propos* in many cases. No greater mistake can be made than to conclude, even after long and frequent inharmonies have occurred in married life, that they are necessarily unfitted for each other. That they may be unfitted for wedlock is true. The divine harmony that should exist in the hearts of those who wish to be everything in the world to each other, and especially with those, who, loving children, desire to make their home blossom with these little rosebuds of heaven, may not, indeed, belong to the ordinary marriage; but change the relationship of these persons, and the knowledge of each other's nature which, perchance, has come through their very differences, may have fitted them for lifelong comradeship with the greatest possible happiness and affections.

Teach young men and women, first of all, not to be afraid of each other; no greater libel can be uttered against a man than mothers make when they impress upon their daughters the necessity of having a *chaperon*.

There is no such thing as friendship between men and women allowed by society; you must either be related or married to the man you know intimately, and, because of this, women are robbed of a friendship which would go far toward fitting them for marriage, and men are cheated out of one of the sweetest of all relationships, namely, a woman friend.

Little has been written which throws light and understanding on the affections and the attractions of man. Reason seems to play no particular part; in fact, they are born and continue to exist in defiance of all reason, and perhaps the greatest sacrifices known are those which have been made upon the altars of affection and love; and the strange part is that they were never looked upon as sacrifices, but were the spontaneous offering of a heart whose highest joy found expression in giving, rather than in receiving. Not infrequently the object of the affection has been wholly unconscious of the gift, and, in too many cases, quite as indifferent to it.

Men and women are not governed, as a rule, by the same law; it is impossible to say that what is right and best for one is equally so for the other. Male and female differ in temperament and character quite as much as they do in physical appearance and formation; man, generally, being the positive, and woman the negative; that is to say, man is the assertive and woman the receptive. While this is the general rule, there is, at the same time, an enormous number of exceptions to it. These elements, probably, have been emphasized by education and circumstance, and through the past centuries man has taken the position of being first in intellect and general capacity. He has moved on his way with a direct line of action marked out; everybody and everything being expected to respond to it. He is, by nature, sympathetic, but not responsive;

his reasoning faculties are more pronounced, but his intuitive and perceptive faculties less so. He is more persistent in purpose, but is susceptible to high influences which may, perhaps, change the entire career of his life, when appealed to from the more selfish or emotional side.

Woman stands, to-day, undeveloped intellectually, but ready to take her part in the great race of life. Thus far she has followed, rather than led, in all departments of human interests; and, through lack of opportunity, has failed to originate much in the realm of ideas. Perhaps this may be due to the fact that man has absorbed some of her intuitive powers, and put into active practice much that he has received through her keener perceptions. The present civilization, however, marks an epoch in the career of woman which is destined to carry the entire race forward to such a point as has never before been revealed.

The century about dawning upon us will be a distinctly competitive one, wherein the intellectual woman will meet the intellectual man, and, sex being wholly ignored, a marriage of achievements will be one of the recognized standards. The day for man's work being well paid, and woman's work underpaid, is fast fading into the twilight, and another day follows on its footsteps in which the work only is recognized regardless of the hands that may have performed it.

In bringing men and women together into the closer relationship of life, there has been, and always will be, almost endless difficulty resulting therefrom until the legitimate sphere of each is recognized.

There should be an acceptance of the rights of each and, the personal sphere being kept intact, the many dangers that now result from the subjection of the will of one to that of the other will be largely avoided and overcome. This, however, can never be done until woman has become as self-supporting and as independent as man; then, when the two come together for the making of a home, it will be for the highest purposes only. Independence being thus developed in woman, the result is respect, and the object of her life becomes something more than simply to marry and marry well. To such an one the mere fact that a man has a certain position, which wealth or circumstance may have bestowed upon him, will not then, as now, play so prominent a part in the settlement of social relations; for, being independent, she will have as much to offer, from her side of the question, as has the man, and there will be no merging of one interest so absolutely into the other as to lose sight of the one altogether; but there will be an union of two interests, the personality of which will be distinctive and the accomplishment mutual. This will not destroy, as some persons declare, the tender characteristics of woman, but will serve to develop her powers and round them out. If her judgment and ability be more, her sympathies will not be the less, although, possibly, guided in their expressions by a greater wisdom; and while there may be less children born from such unions, they will, through more favorable conditions, and a clearer observance of the laws of nature, stand forth as the result of a higher state of civilization.

In the present system of life, children *happen* to be born. Conceived under conditions of excess and irresponsibility, they are regretted, and their birth is too often looked upon as the result of an indiscretion, instead of being the culmination of all that is highest and best in life. The responsibilities of fatherhood and motherhood are too easily accepted, and as easily laid down. If the child of the future is to embody the elements of a higher manhood, it will be the result of the intelligent father and mother; the foundation of this being the observance of those laws which relate to a higher association of two individuals. Every child should be the result of mutual desire; and that desire should only be accepted when all the so-called lower conditions which relate to health, surroundings and circumstances, have been fully recognized. This problem, like all others, should be a matter of the most intelligent consideration; it ought to be understood by the youths of the land, and not left, as it has been, to a stumbling upon results, so disastrous in their nature, and which, in many cases, might have been wholly avoided. But coming down to present-day conditions, and dealing with the subject from a stand-point which will appeal to the practical minded, we have to say, that very few people know much, if anything, about themselves, their own natures or their emotions, and far less in regard to those of others with whom they are brought in contact. Circumstances and individuals induce conditions which appear, for the moment, almost overpowering, are accepted as the final desire of the spirit, and entered in upon, with solemn vows, sanctified by both church and state, for an eternity. No sooner, however, is this contract entered into than its insufficiency is realized. Disappointment is felt on both sides, and, since there is little or no remedy for the condition, life is continued in a dissatisfied or apathetic state. The divorce court, it is true, is constantly called into requisition, and crimes and vices are often assumed by one or both parties, in order to break bonds which, had there been more intelligence in the beginning, would never have been made. But where there is one advertisement of social and marital woes there are, perhaps, thousands of persons who bear the cross of sorrow, and who move among their fellows making neither sign nor sound. The world should be full of health and happiness, and it will be when intelligence governs the expression of the emotions.

Magnetic attraction is the cause of a large number of the unfortunate marriages of the present day. That subtle influence, so little understood, which goes out from one person to another finds a response, and directly the two are swung out upon this current of magnetic attraction, which, ungoverned by intelligence, dulls the intuitions, silences the reason and completely prevents, for the time being, at least, that action of the higher self. Sometimes, when the current is repelled by misunderstanding, a gleam of the real character is momentarily apparent, and each will recognize their mutual unfitness for the other, and are prone, for the moment, to take a decisive step which, if done, would probably prevent subsequent mistakes; but the instant that these magnetic elements again assert themselves all this is obliterated and forgotten, or, if remembered, the reason is silenced by "it will be all right after we are married," which, by the way, is seldom, if ever, the case.

This magnetism referred to is a purely physical and not a spiritual element; it is, consequently, more apparent and assertive in youth, but, later on, when the character is more fully formed and the individual spirit is in a greater state of activity, it has less power, because it has become dominated by the spirit itself. Magnetism is the essence of the chemicals of the human body; when it finds like elements to which it responds, they complete what is called a magnetic attraction, and, so long as one magnetism becomes nearly a complement to the other, so long the individuals are held together. The moment the chemical affinity ceases between these elements the interest in the individual begins to wane, and finally dies out altogether, making that, which was a desired object, unsatisfactory and insufficient, there being no higher emotion called into play by and through such associations. Magnetic conditions being thus outlived, the individuals feel little or no interest in each other, and, whatever the external appearance, each goes out in other directions, and, perchance, may find a spiritual affinity which the exigencies of society will not allow. Thus a life of deception is begun, neither being honest enough to admit the fact, but one or both insisting in words, at least, that there is no change in their feelings whatever. The careworn faces, unhappy lives and unfortunate results of such associations only serve to prove too plainly the truth of this statement, namely, that marriages which are but the result of magnetic attraction carry the elements of death with them, and are bound to fringe the pathway of life, if continued, with sorrow and disease. Then, again, there are many marriages that are founded upon an intellectual appreciation one for the other, where magnetic attraction does not exist to any great degree; but where reason takes control, and says: "this marriage will be a good thing from a worldly point of view." Consequently every other consideration, which appears to be of a purely sentimental order, is ignored, and the material benefits accruing from such an alliance, which society is appointed to sanction with an approving smile, is received and accepted.

There is no more disgusting sight in the haunts of vice and wickedness than that in which a young girl is seen to marry a man possibly twice her age, in whom she has not really the slightest interest, save for his money and position. The sale of virtue in the markets, going on night after night, is, if possible, less reprehensible, and yet, society decries and ostracizes the one, and accepts and approves the other. The state makes laws against the former, and yet, by other laws, sanctions the latter. Thus morality becomes simply a hollow form, regulated by the law of society, which is as unjust in its application as it is partial in its judgment.

Two persons of like intelligence will often see how, by a union of forces, they are able to accomplish practical results. Mentally, they are upon similar planes of development, and their emotional natures being well in hand, they are able to force all their demands, so that they shall conserve to a given point. Such arrangements are called "intellectual marriages;" it might be added that they were formed for business purposes only, since the bringing together of property interests, the uniting of two great names, and the union of social positions, are the only concomitants. If the lines of action laid down in the beginning can be carefully carried out to the end, as is often the case, there will be no bad results attendant upon such a marriage. This marriage is one in which everything is left out, save purely worldly and mercenary interests, which, to the practical minded are, after all, the only important points for consideration; if, however, one or both depart from the original plan, and allow other attributes to assert themselves, trouble, disease and disgust are bound to follow. Thus it is that scandals in high life, among persons of education and ordinary good sense, outrival, in revolting detail, like conditions in lower spheres, plainly evidencing that those of the highest intellects not infrequently make the most grievous mistakes. However valuable the intellect may be, in all the departments of human life, it is certain that, in bringing two individuals together who should walk side by side through life and satisfactorily perform its duties, something beyond mere mental perception and judgment is necessary.

Then there is another class of persons, belonging to the more ideal order of life, who assume to be, and doubtless feel that they are more spiritually minded than the majority of mankind; they put their feet upon what is called earthly attraction and seek a spiritual affinity wherein they hope to find a responsive association which shall embody fondest hopes. But the strangest thing is that such a person seems to know exactly who his spiritual affinity is; and, with the changing variations of his life, passes from one personality to another, finding, at best, only the temporary fulfillment of his idea. Great sacrifices are often made, and much suffering endured; but, there being only an undefined purpose in the mind of the individual, he apparently knows not what he seeks and, consequently, is never certain of having found the object. Such lives are full of sadness and disappointment, and are usually the result of unhealthy physical conditions which place the spirit out of relationship with its only means of expression.

The most complete marriage is where physically, mentally and spiritually two individuals are responsive to each other; they may differ in temperaments, manner of education and social position, but if there be that magnetic responsiveness existing between them as a *whole*, they are bound to be happy in their associations, united in their purposes, and the outcome of such marriages successful in their result. No such union can be formed, however, save upon the plane of a complete understanding, first of one's self and then of the object sought. This marrying to get acquainted after marriage, and looking upon that event as having the power to eliminate great discrepancies of nature which appear beforehand, is all a mistake. Marriage should be a consummation of that which has been undertaken through the guiding power of wisdom and love, and, when the storms of life come and dangers are at hand, such natures will draw nearer and closer, and not be separated by any worldly or contending influences. Distance or separation of any kind, sickness, or any of the fatalities of life, will not be of sufficient strength to build a barrier between them. Temptations from within or without will pass by unnoticed and unrealized; for they have built their foundations upon a rock, and, in the complete responsiveness of their natures, have a strength which defies all of the opposing elements of life. No individuality is sacrificed or lost; there is a *union* of two forces, not the destruction of one or an absorption of the other. Each relies upon itself, and yet has the interests of the other fully in view; and a confidence, faith and trust abides in each heart, making life impregnable to all attacks. A union of this character is, in the highest sense, a true marriage, utopian though it may seem in the light of the present day, where pride and selfishness usurp the place that higher sentiments should occupy.

The onward march of civilization, leveling, as it does, shams in every form, is bound, in the end, to do battle with the hollow mockeries that infest the pathway of progress; and, at last, lead humanity to that goal where the highest stands in noble superiority over and above those baser elements in human nature, which have too long governed the expression of that which is grandest and best; but it will not be until man and woman stands upon the platform of equality, where to each there is a just allotment of smiles and frowns, and where each, performing his or her part, shall receive an emolument commensurate one with the other. Not that man, because he is a man, shall hold a position of superiority over and above what his attainments merit, or because woman as a woman shall either be placed upon a pedestal or hurled down to the depths of endless misery on account of mistakes which, when committed by a man, are passed over with scarcely a word of censure.

A man, to-day, may do about as he pleases, especially if he be circumspect, although the world may know that his life is regretable; and, while it shrugs its shoulders, says, half apologetically, "he is no worse than his fellows," and accepts him. But when a woman, no matter what the circumstance, oversteps a certain limit, there is no anathema too bitter for society to hurl at her, and no judgment too severe for it to visit upon her. Her shortcomings are never passed over by the "sowing of wild oats" theory, but she is expected to be, like Cæsar's wife, above suspicion. And if, perchance, her name should catch the shadow, those who have stood between her and the sun will be the very first to condemn and ostracize her. Society puts woman at a great disadvantage by placing her at so high an altitude, or by casting her down to so low a depth. As honesty, truthfulness and justice are the same, whether in the heart of man or woman, so should morality be; and what is right for one is right for the other. No man has the authority to demand from the woman he is about to marry a purer or a cleaner record than he himself is prepared to show; and if the scarlet letter of prostitution is branded upon the breast of woman so also should it be imprinted upon the breast of man. Society has no right to open her gilded salons to one while it shuts the door in the face of the other.

We cannot leave this subject without saying, what must be apparent to every careful observer, that mistakes of whatever kind do not necessarily involve a depravity of nature, and, if one must judge at all, it should be with the cleanest possible perception. To bring this subject to a close, we can but say that the entire solution of the social problem depends upon enforcing this law of equality, above referred to, and the highest possible education for all concerned, so that its application may be more fully comprehended. Something more than a mere pleasurable alliance or a successful union, from a wordly point of view, must be recognized, and above all this rises the empire of the spirit, into whose realms every man and woman must enter if they hope to find peace and happiness in the end. No benefits however great, no position however brilliant, can be given in payment for the loss of that spiritual recognition which, when once sensed, allies itself with time and eternity.

Where are the highest proofs of love found?

In the mutualities of love.

PART XV.

THE SPIRITUAL IN LITERATURE.

THE SPIRITUAL IN LITERATURE.

(Entered according to Act of Congress, in the year 1898, by AUGUSTA W. FLETCHER, M. D.,
in the office of the Librarian of Congress at Washington.)

The history of civilization is marked by the potent power that literature has always exercised over and upon the development of all ages. Science, mechanics and art, which are so many departments of the human mind, have each been prominent factors, as they ever must be, in the development of all that is possible to man; but the sphere which literature has filled has been, perhaps, more comprehensive and far-reaching than any of these, since development in the above departments is easily superseded by more advanced revelations, and earlier acquirements are relegated to partial forgetfulness. But in literature this is not the case. Whatever is said wisely to one age bears a relative connection to every other; and, while great strides may be made in various directions, the backward trail is never lost, and the student finds more pleasure in reveling in past achievements than in contemplating future glories. Consequently the philosophers, a thousand years from now, are destined to be, if possible, more alive and present, as active agents in the development of thought, than in the age in which they lived and worked. This, perhaps, is due to the fact that all great minds have stepped beyond the limits which are usually placed upon the realms of thought, and, unknown to themselves, entered into that of the spirit and gathered much that is beautiful and lasting.

There has always been a practical vein running through every age and time, which has exerted its influence, and to which the majority have been responsive. The founding of nations, the building of cities, and the forming of great enterprises have all been essentially due to this, and those who were therein engaged had little time and, possibly, less inclination to turn their thoughts to other things.

The successful general, though possessed of an artistic temperament, would fail in his leadership were he to give any part of his time to the unfolding of the more ideal side of his nature, while a great writer, who is able to recall, with startling accuracy, events upon which the destiny of the world has turned, would, without doubt, have played a sorry part had that destiny depended upon his individual connection with it. No matter how diversified the nature, there are certain departments in which it is more supreme than in others. Inclinations which it has are so much better adapted to the general drift of the individual, that it is only through the development of these that great attainments are ever realized; and, while there are many lesser possibilities inherent in the nature, these can best be called the shoots growing upon the vine that the wise gardener clips off so as to give greater strength to the perfection of that which remains. Every great nature, which courts the admiration of the world by the magnificence of its attainments, has many other possibilities within, and, had they been developed, they would have been secondary only to those to which it has given the strength of its life. It is argued, we know, by some, that it is wiser to partially develop the many possibilities of life rather than to sacrifice the many to the one or two which are more apparent; that while we shall attain a lesser degree of excellence in one direction, we shall, none the less, gain a greater development in another which is salutary in its effect. This might be true if there was but one life to live; but when it is understood that there is plenty of time for everything, and that lives follow on in rapid succession until all demands are satisfied, it can be readily seen that the outworking of one purpose at a time, gaining all the experience that is possible, is the better course.

The great writers of the past, like those of the present, were so constituted that they lived within, and yet above, the general drift of the world. The barrier between the mind and the spirit is, in such natures, more easily penetrated, and a view of a possible humanity is thereby gained.

Not infrequently the spirit of prophesy speaks through the burning words of writer and poet, the full import of which he but dimly understands. His spirit is lifted above the sordid conditions of earth, and revels in a conscious spiritual life freed from all that weighed him down. No wonder, then, that he appears to be a dreamer, to possess an imperfect mind, and to be unfitted for a close contact with those who, dwelling in immediate relationship with earthly interests, are too selfish and dull to enter into or comprehend even in part, the magnitude of his ideas. And yet, the unrecognized truth that they contain is only a prophesy which the coming age is bound to realize and accept.

If more attention was paid to the impressions that the poets, for instance, have given us we should have a very different and a more wholesome view of life than we have. But the world seems to feel that those natures in whom the poetical elements predominate are never to be taken quite seriously; and while rhyme and rhythm are admired, the thought running through them is too often lost sight of, and ignored altogether. True, in the great epochs of the world, they are called upon to play an important part, and their words, filled with enthusiasm and prophesy, fall upon willing ears, only in turn to be soon forgotten. It is our purpose to show that the great writers have always been more or less at touch with the spiritual world, that the conditions of life existing in the realms above have been reflected, to a certain degree, upon their minds, and that they have endeavored to reproduce a picture most tangible to them in moments of inspired thought.

Thus Shakespeare, Shelly, Lytton, Longfellow, and many others, have all been instruments in the hands of the spiritual world. If their works are carefully examined by the astute observer it will be found that they have suggested far more than they have written; that an undercurrent of thought is apparent, and, while at times almost concealed by the exigencies of the age for which they have been writing, none the less it carries the mind onward to heights which pierce the clouds, and loses itself in the beauty of another world.

Nor can this be said to have happened by chance; if

one part of the work is to be taken seriously then it should all be taken in the same way. As, for instance, in the works of William Shakespeare, a greater genius than whom, in his line, the ages have failed to produce, we find a continual allusion to the life after death. The presence and guardianship of spirits, and the outworking of human passions, are each played upon, quite as much by the unseen as the seen.

Indeed, the *motif* of more than one of the plays of this prolific writer is based upon the spiritual idea altogether; and, while historical events, circumstances and traditions are woven in with wonderful *finesse*, the central idea stands out all the more boldly by contrast. That the unthinking follow these great tragedies from beginning to end without perceiving their purpose argues nothing, for the general mind accepts incidents instead of analyzing motives.

The play of Hamlet particularly illustrates our thought. Eliminate the ghost of Hamlet's father, and, while you have remaining all the historical facts, the interest goes out with it; and yet, all the personages in that great tragedy seem oblivious to the thought that it suggests, as have thousands of others who have watched those events enacted on the stage of a theatre for their instruction and delectation. Shakespeare must have realized that the dead king was not removed from contact with material things, that he was cognizant of what had occurred since he left the earth, and that these events produced an impression upon his mind revolting in its nature; and he was, therefore, uneasy in his grave, or, rather, in that life beyond the grave.

The human side was influenced in death, as in life, by earthly events, and, seeing that his position had been affected, and believing that great wrong had been done to himself, he appears again and again to his son, demanding, from a purely earthly standpoint, that his wrongs should be righted.

Hamlet was a sensitive youth; he lived apart from his kind, had been a dreamer of dreams, and was susceptible to the influences of his surroundings; all of which are the concomitants of a mediumistic organization. What more natural, then, that his father, seeking some one through whom he could outwork his outraged will, appeared to this youth, and, in speaking to him, manifested a knowledge of all that had happened, and demanded that a certain form of retribution should follow. There seems to have been no question concerning the genuineness of the apparition, as there could be none as to the truthfulness of the statements made. Acting, therefore, upon the communications thus received, Hamlet plans for the carrying out of such purposes as the spirit insisted upon, in all of which he finally succeeds.

A more complete illustration of the theory of the Spiritualist cannot be found in history than is unfolded in this tragedy, in which is demonstrated the survival of the spirit after the death of the body, the retention of its interest in human affairs, and the ability to follow them, together, under proper conditions, with the power to communicate with those in the earth life, not having necessarily changed in character or purpose through passing the portals of death.

Shakespeare must have believed this or he could not have written of it with such directness. It undoubtedly was his intention to have taught precisely this lesson, for the non-acceptance of which the world cannot be much blamed, since, after witnessing all these manifestations, following their guidance, and proving their truthfulness, Hamlet, himself, seems to have realized nothing of their interior import; for, in the very midst of these exciting scenes, he questions the facts in this wise: "To be or not to be." He speaks of death, and expresses his dread thereof, as if in the return of his father he had not seen the solution of the problem, and the unveiling of the mystery. And in his words, the voice of the world is heard.

Again, in the play of Richard III., the vision that comes to haunt his dreams embodies the same spiritual idea; while, in the still greater play of Julius Cæsar, the spirit of prophecy, on the plains of Philippi, only serves to more fully illustrate this thought. In fact, you will scarcely find one of the dramas from this master-hand in which there will not be some suggestion of the spiritual world as it is understood by the intelligent and spiritually minded of the present day; and if we were to name the works in which a comprehensive illustration of the spiritual philosophy can be found, the plays of Shakespeare, carefully studied, and their full meaning understood, would stand first among our selection; for in them will be found so great a preponderance of these ideas that they cannot fail to suggest a line of teaching which the thinkers of the present day are endeavoring to give to the world.

Nor are these intimations of visitations from the spiritual world confined to this profound and prolific writer alone. Other men of great genius have, seemingly, caught glimpses of the great beyond, and transcribed them for the benefit of succeeding generations, and, turning their eyes heavenward, have beheld the dark clouds of doubt pierced, here and there, by rays of hope that have served to strengthen their weary hearts. The writers more modern than these masterhands have felt, in a similar way, what they have so graphically depicted, the expression of which has depended largely upon their own personality and the varying moods in which the thought finds them.

The "Strange Story," by Lord Lytton, is an epitome of spiritual experiences, rather than a novel, upon which the lovers of the mysterious have been able to feed and stimulate their imagination. This book, like all his other works, is remarkable not alone in what it says, but in the possibilities it intimates. No more inspiring words can be found in the English language than the closing pages of the last chapter, which compel the feeling that, if the author had only continued, he would have revealed truths of far greater importance than have, heretofore, enlisted the attention of the human mind. In fact, the preface, itself, deals with man's life in such a way as to apportion and classify it into departments, thereby rendering its expressions more susceptible of analysis, and complete comprehension.

It is accepted, by all thinkers of any degree of intelligence, that, as he states, there are three lives in the one life, the body and the mind, important factors though they are, being subservient to the great central impulse, namely, the soul, the destiny of which is beyond the comprehension of the wisest. Later on, he says that love teaches there is something of nobler value than the mind; yet surely it cannot be the mere body. What is it, then, if not the continuance of that something which philosophy declines to recognize, namely, again, the soul.

It will be seen, throughout all of this, that an attempt to lift the conception of man from the realm of material thought into that of the spiritual is made; awakening, at the same time, a realization of the fact that the events of a life-time are important only so far as they are relegated, in their results, to the domain of the human soul, for whose perfection and development they are permitted to exist. This is quite independent of any theological interpretation, and, seemingly, takes the mind into the domain of Naturalism, where, without doubt, the ultimate religion of mankind will be found.

One is impressed with the occult in this "Strange Story," and is almost compelled to recognize the demonstration of a mysterious power as a possible verity, even though it be entirely without the range of human experience. This is, perhaps, partly due to the strong hand of the author, and is also confirmed by an inward responsiveness.

The soul of man is able to recognize as true much that the mind, through its imperfect education, would reject; and, yet, who shall say that, through a combination of the mysterious and subtle forces in nature, it be not possible to make the invisible visible, and the silence audible? Surely, not the students of natural science; for so far have they penetrated the regions of the unknowable that many religiously inclined are prone to think that such explorations border upon the profane; and, without doubt, the time will come when that science which has done so much for the world, during the past century, will drop the very prejudices which it so largely condemns in its opponents now, and cease laughing at what it is pleased to call the supernatural, and the wild vagaries of diseased imaginations. Then, perhaps, they will be able to answer the question that this author raises as to who shall console the mourner "whose dead is dead forever." But, perhaps, by that time, they will have realized that there are no dead, and that death forever is one of the impossibilities of nature.

Be that as it may, a "Strange Story" will well repay any reader who is at all interested in the so-called mysterious; and suggest, at least, a line of thought as to future possibilities which will assist, at any rate, not alone in a fuller comprehension of a life here, but in the hereafter as well. Generations that are to come will read this book, and find in it a world of hidden meaning which, in the light of to-day, is passed over unrecognized. We refrain from a more extensive reference to the works of this author, since it is only our purpose to indicate that this and other writers were alive, even in their time, to the questions which are enlisting the minds of the thinkers of the present day.

The American poet, Longfellow, has wisely and rightly been called the "comforter," since his songs appeal to the heart, and, through them, the spirit of consolation breathes her sweet and divine influence.

"There are more guests at the table than the host invited" instinctively suggests the presence of unseen visitors, whose affections are still strong enough to draw them to the scenes of their earthly life.

> The stranger at my fireside cannot see
> The forms I see, nor hear the sounds I hear;
> He but perceives what is: while unto me
> All that has been is visible and clear.

—carries with it the possibility of the development of the perceptive faculties to that degree whereby these beings can be seen and recognized.

In the "Psalm of Life," the indestructibility of the soul is absolutely asserted:

> Dust thou art, to dust returnest,
> Was not spoken of the soul.

Could a more emphatic recognition of the something that is beyond both mind and matter be made, than is done in these lines? But, as if to carry a still fuller acceptance of spiritual presence, he says, in the "Footsteps of Angels":

> Ere the evening lamps are lighted,
> And, like phantoms, grim and tall,
> Shadows from the fitful firelight
> Dance upon the parlor wall;
>
> Then the forms of the departed
> Enter at the open door;
> The beloved, the true hearted,
> Come to visit me once more.

If these words are to be taken seriously, or with any degree of authority, they must mean precisely what they say; and the forms of our departed loved ones do enter the open door, as the cares of the day depart, and hold converse with us; thus robbing death of all its terrors, and making the open door of the grave an entrance to that world, the limits of which are past the comprehension of man; and yet, all the while, revealing the immortality of love which forgets not, but seeks still to guard and bless its own.

If this idea was accepted there would be less sadness in the world than there is to-day; and fathers, and mothers, and friends, when they fold the tired hands to rest, and close the weary eyes in the long slumber, would feel that but one volume in life's great book had been closed, and that another, whose words human eyes may not read, had been opened in its place. Harriet Beecher Stowe, whose mind was particularly impressionable, writes of the spiritual world as being in close proximity to this,

> "It lies around us like a cloud, a world we may not see."

And her brother, the Rev. Henry Ward Beecher, whose service for humanity has not, as yet, been recognized, said, upon more than one occasion, that he had been lifted into an ecstatic state, where the spiritual world seemed about him everywhere and he a part of it.

The "Gates Ajar," "Old Lady Mary," and numberless other works entirely outside the realms of modern Spiritualism, have, in their teaching, inculcated certain phases of spiritual law which are at variance with theologies, both past and present, but in accord with the experience of every student of the occult.

PART XVI.

HAS MAN LIVED MORE LIVES THAN ONE?

PART XVI

USED MORE LIKELY THAN ONCE

HAS MAN LIVED MORE LIVES. THAN ONE?

(Entered according to Act of Congress, in the year 1893, by AUGUSTA W. FLETCHER, M. D., in the office of the Librarian of Congress at Washington.)

However many problems the intelligence of man may solve, he can but hope, in his present stage of development, to approximate an answer to the question, "What is Life?"

He may wring from nature many of her secrets, harness the great forces of the universe in such chains that they become the servants of his will, read the story of the stars, catch the whisperings of the infinite, and learn from the ever-open book of nature, laws of great value to himself and his kind. But when he enters into the inner temple of self, and seeks to solve the mystery of his own existence, the laws of his life, and the mighty secrets that the future holds in its keeping, he stands aghast; and, instead of pressing onward, too often falls back upon those questionable theories which the lesser minds of the past have left as a record of their incomplete research. Backward the mighty waves of eternity roll, losing themselves in the measureless limits of a distant past; forward the mighty tide of life sweeps on its way, carrying everything before it, until systems, kingdoms, principalities and powers have crumbled into dust; and yet, individual life remains standing in proud superiority over and above the fading scenes of earthly existence.

That man, seemingly, holds to the present only, is to be expected; his thoughts, activities, ambitions, all relate to this, the present sphere of his conscious life. That he holds within himself the sum of all that has been, counts for nothing, since he is unable to unite the experiences of the past, with the actualities of the present, all seeming to be the concomitants of this life, which have sprung into existence with all their forces and abilities at one and the same time. The past is related to him only through the lives and experiences of others. He is not able to see that he must, individually, have grown through every phase of civilization that marks the history of the world, before he could possibly have reached his present status of development. He, therefore, speaks of the past as a thing apart from himself, of those who lived therein as being less fortunate than is he, and, with an egotism born of an undeveloped nature, reverently thanks God that he lives in the present age; forgetting, that those who lived in the age just past, were equally as thankful that they had escaped the century preceding them, and that those who are to be born a hundred years from now, will, with greater fervor still, appreciate the blessings and opportunities of their time, which will be the result of added experiences and larger wisdom.

Man always feels that the future is his; that whatever there is in time or eternity he is bound, one day, to absorb; and never, for one moment, does he imagine that he will cease to hold about the same relationship to persons and things that he holds now. Difficult as it is to conceive of time continuing endlessly, it is far more difficult to arrive at that point when there shall be no time, and life ceases to retain its active existence and connection with the mighty forces of the universe. Why, then, if man holds that he is related to all that is to be, does he not recognize that a like connection must have existed with all that has been; and that he, in arriving at his present stage of development, must have been at oneness with the law of progress; and, as an intelligent entity, have passed through the different gradations of development in order to attain unto his present status? In other words, if man is to live in the eternity of the future he must also have lived in the forever of the past; and, instead of being an especial creation, set down in the midst of to-day, with a direct impulse to carry on the work of the world as he finds it, he is an epitome of all experiences that have been; the present form of life adding only one more phase to those that already make up the sum of his personal individuality.

We hold that man, as man, has always existed. Positive in his purposes, varied in physical form, but continuous in his development; and has attained unto the *ego*, within himself, through the natural evolution of his spirit, his association with human life, and the unfoldment of all those spiritual and mental qualities that make him what he is. The difference between the unfolded nature which is responsive to all the conditions of life that surround it, and that nature which moves in the narrow sphere of its own individual conceit, is due to the fact that the first has gone through all the lower conditions, and used them as steps in the stairway of life, whereby he has climbed up to his present height; while the second is stumbling along the way, with little or no comprehension of a higher purpose, but with a realization of every physical and personal result; and he will continue to climb until all the dross is eliminated from his nature, and he stands, side by side, with the highest. Thus is the justice of heaven and the wisdom of God made manifest.

Those who seemingly court the admiration of the world through and by their present development, are, as yet, children who have begun to learn the alphabet of life, whose mysteries are as a sealed book before them. They, too, will pass on from height to height, from glory to glory, until they shall have lost all that petty personality that mars, even now, the natures of the great, and enter in upon that wider sphere of action wherein their labors will find the highest expression, in a complete forgetfulness of self. They may find that in the spheres of the spiritual world alone, and, if so, they will abide therein; they may, however, accomplish it by returning to the earth again, and yet, again, taking upon themselves human form for the specific purpose of acquiring another line of experience; and, each time, return to human life a more developed man than before, although not always so appearing to the casual observer. Such return is dependent upon having exhausted all that one set of conditions held, before any new duties could be undertaken or assumed.

Thus the men of to-day have moved through similar scenes a thousand years ago, and the sense of familiarity found in persons, and landscapes, is but a remnant of their past, which persistently projects itself upon their present consciousness, and forms, as it were, an incomplete memory of by-gone events.

Be it understood, we hold that all relations existing in the present are essentially of a comparatively temporary nature; not that we mean by the word temporary that they will cease to exist before they shall have served their purposes, but that the purposes themselves sustain no permanent relation to the greater events of time and eternity. In fact, a life-time on earth is often sufficient to live out the relationships which that life has attracted to itself. Parents, children, friends, and, in fact, all the concomitants of a life-time, are, seemingly, born only to die; and their true value will be found, not in their existence, but in the effect that they have produced upon themselves and others. The only relation that has the element of continuity will be found when spirit responds to spirit, which seldom, if ever, exists upon this stage of life.

We do not mean that human affections are hollow and valueless, or that they end with death; on the contrary, they are, for the time being, of the greatest possible importance; and they continue beyond the change, just so long as they serve the purposes for which they were created. But there comes a time when they are outlived, outgrown, and stronger attractions are called into existence, which assert themselves and thus create an entirely different condition. Nor does this militate against the value of the former. The friends of your childhood were important to you, and served the purpose of making those days golden, bright and happy. They, in fact, paved the way for the stronger friendships of manhood which came after them as a fitting complement to the influence that they had exerted. The friendships of childhood were valuable to their time as were also the friendships of manhood to theirs. They were not the same, they could never be the same, for that law of progress which lives and acts in the spirit of man, is bound to carry it forward in spite of everything, and, though it may pass over the graves of past loves and dead ambitions, it only does so to bring him to the resurrection morn, wherein those earlier loves which were only possibilities, shall be found blossoming into realities, while he, having gathered spiritual strength from each experience, has grown into a more appreciable state of development, and, although enlarged in his view and understanding, seemingly sustains about the same outward relationship to them. At this point, he will see that there have been no accidents and no mistakes; that the loss and gain which, momentarily, shadowed his path, and the misfortunes that ever have and ever will exert their depressing influence, were all factors employed in the building up of that spiritual self-hood which now stands forth crowned with the light of divine approbation, not as the conclusion to all of life's purposes, but, rather, the closing of one volume to open a still more important one.

He who looks out over the sea of humanity, with its heights and depths, its blessings and curses, no matter how elastic his reasoning, cannot assert that human beings are justly governed or apportioned, if all things

HAS MAN LIVED MORE LIVES THAN ONE? 255

end with the present life. Inequality forces itself upon the attention until theologians themselves are compelled, when facing them, and an explanation is demanded, to reply, "these are the mysteries of God, veiled from human sight, to be made clear only on the judgment day." And, perhaps, this answer conveys as little harm as any we can suggest, since, after all, they have said, in other words, "We know not why things are as they are, and man must wait for time and intelligence to furnish an explanation." But to suppose that there shall be no growth toward this knowledge, no approximating toward this reality, is to ignore the existence of the great law of progress which theologians, and theology, alike, have always endeavored to repudiate.

To state the position plainly, we have but to say that the soul of man is a direct emanation from the divine spirit, is the result of the connection between the soul, and matter, and, every time this connection is resumed, a different expression of soul-life is made upon the earth plane, and each time more perfectly than before. That this will continue as the action of a law upon which perfected life is dependent, must be recognized, if our conclusions are to be accepted, and that it will continue throughout the realm of a higher life, in much the same way, until each has eliminated every trace of the processes of life, and, thereby, given to the soul its direct individuality.

This is in direct consonance with the law of physical evolution. Whatever the condition of the planet may be, it is the result of the sunshine and storm through which it has passed. The high state of cultivation existing in the present day is absolutely due to the cyclone and tornado that have marked the history of the past; and, if the old has passed away, and all things become new again, it is in the newness of form, instead of the newness of creation, so far as the elements employed are concerned. The nebulous and glacial periods, and, in fact, all the conditions, of whatsoever nature or kind, have been like so many fingers moulding and shaping the planet into its present form. Nor is this work yet completed; every year marks the action of this moulding process, and will continue, far beyond the conception of man.

A flower blooms on the table before me, and, at first sight, seems to live apart from the rest of the world. It is difficult, for the moment, to imagine that it has grown up from the damp ground, nurtured by the earth, and kissed by the sun, until it stands revealed a thing of beauty, and a joy forever. And yet, even as I look, it begins to wither and fade, and, perchance, ere the day is done, its connection with the floral kingdom is severed, and it returns to nature's laboratory with the effect of the flower-life upon it, to be worked over again, and then to enter in upon a higher phase of existence. Its identity as a flower has ceased, as that was not its ultimate; but the refining results of its short life are found in every particle that it possessed. If the old identity is lost, a newer phase of existence has been born to take its place; and those wise in science will tell you that we are more than foolish to weep over the passing changes of the seasons, over death in any form, since, if the angel of time walks the earth bearing the torch of the destroyer in one hand, she, likewise, carries the hammer of the builder in the other, and uses them both with equal efficiency. What seems like destruction in the world of things, is only the releasing of one power to make room for another, The forest is leveled, and, from its mighty timbers, the town is built; destroyed as a forest, yes; but that destruction is succeeded by such superior conditions that the wise rejoice, and the foolish, alone, regret.

The entire theory of the evolution of matter, as taught by Darwin, is duplicated in the evolution of spirit; the only difference being, that the scientist declared that what appears to be mind or spirit is the result of the physical elements constituting the human body, which, in turn, cease when that body no longer sustains its former relationship with the universe of matter.

The spiritual scientist declares that the evolution of matter is dependent upon, and, is the result of the action of spirit, and that this planet, and every other whereon life exists, is but the school-room in which the spirit is learning the lessons of life; and, when they are completed, it will be transplanted to higher realms of existence. And, without further elaboration, we pass on to the consideration of other phases of this subject.

It must not be understood that the individual spirit is always directly drawn into connection with matter. There are many forms of re-embodiment: some absolute and others partial; and allow us to say, right here, that in the foregoing we are stating the conclusions of advanced spirits as taught in the spiritual world, and we must be uninfluenced by the criticisms of the reader, of whom, in any case, we can but expect that our thoughts will be more suggestive than conclusive, as this subject is not one of logical demonstration, but is, instead, dependent upon spiritual perception for its complete apprehension. Those who are seeking for the light, may find an added ray in these thoughts, while those who have found it, will, at once, be enabled to appreciate their value and worth. We are more than aware that in them will be found an influence which will produce a spirit of unrest and dissatisfaction, one which, invariably, precedes all real growth of the spirit. In fact, the entire object of this book is not to bring peace, but the sword into the world, that is, we must turn the furrow before the seed can be planted; and those who are satisfied with the stubble and cannot realize seed-time and harvest, will, without doubt, look upon our effort as a mistaken and misguided one. The South Sea Islander has but a poor appreciation of the advanced stage of civilized life, and yet, the civilization that he denounces and decries, is destined to accomplish for him and his land, what he individually can never do for either.

Re-embodiment, as above stated, is complete; the spirit has passed through the entirety of one phase of its career, and, finding that it can thus serve its best interests, is, through the subtle law of magnetic attraction, drawn back to the earth again. It will take on a form of life probably the opposite of that which preceded it, and, in turn, will live out, both in this and higher states of existence, a needed development; thus it may return again, and again, and yet again, losing what are called the traces of identity but forever retaining, within itself, the result that has been gained by these successive lives.

You observe that we place man entirely outside of all physical conditions, save those which are made to serve the purposes of the spirit; consequently, what are called traces of identity are, more or less, due to the PERSONALITY of the body, which is quite a different thing; for, under all circumstances, when the spirit is divested of physical conditions, the marks of spiritual identity are more apparent than any physical conditions could be.

One life is all insufficient for the accomplishing of the smallest of those purposes which flit through the human brain in its most inactive moments. No matter how well a life has been lived, how intense the efforts, or how close the application, the unattained rises like a mountain, and stands in strong contrast to the mole-hill above which is written in feeble characters the word, "ACCOMPLISHED." And it is for the outworking of all purposes, that the door is left open through which the vanishing forms of one generation are passing, to admit of the return of another, which will take up the work that has been laid down.

Every returning spirit, before it enters in upon the scenes of earthly life, is attracted, probably, more by the law of chemical affinity than anything else, to such material conditions as will best adapt themselves to its individual requirements, and the experience needed.

Circumstances may have made a man a ruler of men, the outward trappings and signs of office being the envy of his time; and yet, such an one may be of so ignoble a nature as to stand far beneath, in spiritual development, the hireling whose very existence he ignores. Character and spiritual development are the standards, and all things, of whatsoever nature and kind, are made secondary to them; consequently, he who judges by worldly position, wealth or influence can, at best, form but a very superficial conclusion as to what the nature of the man really is. These outward things will as surely pass away as that the sun shines; but those qualities, out of which his spiritual nature is builded, are as abiding as anything in time or eternity; consequently, true judgment is confined to the latter rather than to the former, and upon this we base our conclusions.

The untoward conditions of human life are all efforts that the spirit is making to attain advancement. The drunkard, the murderer, and the thief are what they are by the action of a law which, if understood, would lead to milder judgments, and the employment of better remedies for the amelioration of their condition.

When the apostle said, "judge not," he uttered a most important command; for, from an earthly standpoint, no human being is able to form an impartial or just decision as regards states of human life, which are the outgrowth of the conditions in which they have been nourished and fed, and, for which, they have been constructed to assist some spirit into the light.

To say that the human family, or any part of it, is totally depraved, is to reveal an ignorant mind, and an undeveloped spirit in one's self. Each man and woman is in a state best suited for them at the time, and, whatever the experience that may result therefrom, it is through this, and this alone, that a remedy will be found; so that an entire lifetime may be devoted to the outliving of so-called wicked traits which, in every human being, are temporarily bound to manifest themselves. When this transcends the boundary line that society has laid down by which to protect itself, it curtails the action of individuals, and thus hospitals, prisons, and reformatories are constructed; but those who are confined therein have as much right to their existence as any human being extant. They, in every instance, are necessary elements in the great problem of life, and when the sum of existence is added up, much will be given to the bad that is now withheld, while, perhaps, an equal amount will be taken from the so-called good, because it is not legitimately their own. There is no standard of absolute goodness; and evil, instead of being a positive quality, simply exists because of the absence of good, susceptible, in the passage of time, to the playing of a part which serves to make up concomitants of individual life.

Men are, when viewed from the standpoint of the soul-world, but children, and are no more responsible; what seems to be innate wickedness is simply a portion of the nature that has not yet succumbed to the cultivation of the individual spirit, and is, for the time being, running to weeds. The very life of evil on the soil, demonstrates the possibility of good, which becomes reality the moment that the spirit gains a supreme control over all the departments of life. In other words, bad men are incomplete men; the relationship existing between the spirit, and the body, in which it is living, is only partial; and, wherever the spirit is deficient in its activities, the body, acting independently, asserts itself, and generally in the wrong direction. A man, spiritually, may repudiate and decry a love for liquor, and yet be brought into such relationship with its influence, that the chemical elements of the body will assert themselves over and beyond the authority of the spirit, and before the *ego* is able to conquer this desire, the appetite has satisfied itself, and the harm is done. To such an one, life is one continual harassing regret, and should it end without the appetite being conquered and overcome, the effect would follow the spirit throughout all the earlier conditions of the spiritual life; but when such a spirit returns to the earth again, and is re-embodied, it would swing to the other extreme, and be as noted in that life for its temperance and sobriety, as it had been distinguished in the former one for the opposite; having, thereby, lived out the influence of evil, and expelled from its nature whatever bad effects resulted therefrom. And thus is the evolution of the spirit carried on, until it rises above every earthly power, and becoming absolutely self-centred, governs whatever conditions it is brought in contact with.

It is not possible to indicate the number of incarnations, nor is it important that such indication should be given, since it is the effect produced, rather than the methods employed, that is the subject for consideration.

You may have observed that many persons are noted for their charitable judgment, gentleness of speech and kindly acts, and are entitled to respect for the liberality which they have attained. You would, perhaps, imagine that this position was the result of a life devoted to a study of the higher qualities; but, in nearly every instance, you will find, on taking a retrospective look over the past re-embodiment of such persons, that there have been many times when their actions were most reprehensible and condemnatory; and, for the moment, you are prone to say that no person has the right to assume any superior condition when he has such a past. If you were to stop at different points in this record you would, without doubt, find no element of saving grace; but the result, as is seen in many instances, was for good, consequently, whatever the methods employed, you are bound to admit that there must have been the element of goodness running through them, or, otherwise, the result could not be what it is.

Those who have sinned, and intelligently conquered its influence, are the only ones who can truly understand the sinner; those who have suffered and learned the lesson that sorrow teaches, are alone able to sympathize with the unfortunate, and it is right to say that one life, with all its varying conditions, is but a type of what is the destiny of each life to live out to its uttermost, before the full purpose of earthly living is realized. That is to say, the lowest depths in human nature are all to be lived up to the highest point in human nature; and successive lives, on this earth, is the process by which this purpose is accomplished.

We come now to what is, perhaps, the most difficult

part of our subject, namely, the objections which prejudice and ignorance offer to this idea.

We have, first, on the part of nearly all, a great love of individual life, and the fear that this law will in some way destroy it; that John Smith will not always remain John Smith; that should he return to the earth in any other form and bear any other name, it is proof presumptive, it could not be he, when the name and the attributes relating to John Smith have, in reality, answered the purpose; and returning a thousand years afterward he would bring back these qualities so developed as to make them, and, consequently, himself, unrecognizable.

In an ordinary lifetime, the boy of fifteen is absolutely lost in the intelligent man of forty-five, and you might as well argue against the effect of the passage of time upon the individual, declaring that because he has apparently changed at forty-five from what he was at fifteen, that he never existed at that early age at all, but was always what he appears to be now, as to insist that in the culmination of all past experiences, that necessarily recognizable traces of a former identity should be manifested again. Such, however, is the impracticability of human nature, that it drifts on the current, unconsciously deluding itself with the idea that it is holding on to the same identity all the time, which, in reality, is slipping away as rapidly as possible. Undefined as is the future life to the minds of most people, any explanation of that life which apparently changes the status of the individual, either toward himself or in any of the conditions of life, is rejected without thought or consideration. He knows not what the process of continuous development is, and has no explanation for what has been. He simply wishes to keep himself as he is, while, each moment of time, he is undergoing the process of change, although oblivious to it. Upon the ground of religion he will find every reason to denounce all ideas or theories that are likely to trespass upon the domain which theology has claimed for its own.

This is to be expected; but the thinker, outside, can have no such objection, and, we believe, implicitly, that when science discovers the soul of man, which some day it is bound to do, it will recognize this law of the evolution of the spirit as co-existent with the evolution of matter. Until then, we shall be compelled to wait, as patiently as possible, for the result of this self-same evolution that will bring the scientific mind up to a comprehension of the fact so patent to ourselves.

The most important objections made by the general mind are that all earthly relationship will be ignored, that fathers and mothers will lose their children, and individuals will become so mixed up in the various forms of life, that one will not be able to recognize the other. This, we unhesitatingly affirm, is one of the results to be most desired. All relationships existing in the world are the result of time and circumstance, and bear no relation whatever to eternity; each spirit is independent of each other spirit, and the more rounded out it is the more independent it becomes. The consequence is, that too much stress, altogether, is laid upon the ties which, temporarily, play so important a part in human existence. They are frequently outlived in a short term of years, and those that, in the beginning, were thought to be everlasting and all-enduring, are continually being supplanted by other connections which, for the time, seem as positive as were the former ones; and so on, and on, until the spirit arrives at that point where, becoming self-centred, it is able to stand alone; then, by the law of affinity, those who are at oneness with each other are attracted thereto.

There is no reason to suppose that a child is spiritually yours because circumstances have made you its physical parent. There may not be a single point of harmony between you and the service that you render; the protection that you give, results from duty rather than from any higher nature. Be it remembered, however, that so long as any benefit is to be derived from a recognition of the apparent relationship, thus existing, it will be sustained, and will only cease when the mutual benefit, accruing therefrom, has ended.

Again, the idea held by many that the spirit goes on, and on, to nobler aims and purposes, does not form an objection, as some might think, to our position; since, we hold that the spirit is progressing all the time, only it does not take up that law through the higher realms of spiritual life until it has exhausted whatever this life holds.

To be sure, we are met by the question, "if I have lived through different conditions before, why do I not recall them?" Our answer is, that the understanding of a condition is the memory of that condition; no person is able to realize a state that they have not passed through, while the circumstances of a trivial nature may no longer make even a faint impression upon the mind; yet, the spirit of the condition remains with the individual, and is in evidence as the result of that through which he has passed. Without doubt, if there be any use therein, when the entire circle of earthly life has been compassed, then the spirit will, if it desires, be able to induce any phase of life through which it has passed, and, if it chooses, take it up again.

The Spiritualist insists that a communication between the two worlds is presumptive argument against the law of re-embodiment; but, by so doing, he shows how far away he is from grasping the thought itself, for we do not hold that re-embodiment follows directly after death, but only when the spirit requires that development which it can attain in no other way.

Thus a Spiritualist can receive communications from his spirit friends with perfect surety that they are present with him, and, not until all the attraction existing between them has ceased, and all the purposes of this phase of life, in its continuation in the spiritual world, as well, have been absorbed, will the personality that he knows be dropped and the new one taken on.

But the Spiritualist adds, "Such communication fails to inculcate this idea of re-embodiment, and when my spirit-friends are asked in regard to it, they seem to be in complete ignorance of the law." This forms no argument whatever, since all spirits, in a certain phase, only reach a certain standard of knowledge; and until the moment came that re-embodiment was to take place, the spirit would not, probably, be able to recognize the point for which he was aiming; and, at such a moment his former earthly friend would be in exact relationship with him, and comprehend as fully as he does himself. The spirits of the long-ago are seldom heard from in this age, because they have ceased to exist in the individuality that marked them then, while those who have recently passed out, are ever returning and communicating.

We might go on considering an indefinite number of objections which will present themselves to every mind that is not prepared, through education or development, to absorb this important truth; but we are inclined to state our position rather than to enter in upon any mental combat with any one. Suffice it to say, that after all is said and done, things would remain about the same; growth being necessary for a fuller understanding of whatever might be said.

We would say, in further continuation of our idea, that, through associative influences, spirits gain a vast amount of experience that sometimes renders a complete re-embodiment unnecessary; through uniting themselves with another individual who is passing through phases of earth-life which contain desired lessons, they can gain a result which is beneficial in its effect, and helps to carry them forward.

The controls of mediums are an illustration of this idea. All such controls are allied to their mediumistic instruments by an attraction which draws them into the earth so fully, that, not infrequently, they forget that they are not wholly embodied. They are susceptible to the whole range of human emotions, and, while above the earth, are still within the range of earthly influences. They generally have been associated with such a medium from the hour of his birth, and, usually, remain with him until he changes his sphere of existence. Thus, while they are working for humanity, by their advice and ministration, they are gaining for themselves an experience which is of untold value to them.

Such spirits are usually almost the counterpart of the one with whom they are associated, although there are many exceptions to this statement. Sometimes the influence will be below, and, then, again, above the recognized standard of the medium himself. In the former case much good instruction could be given, and, in the latter, much received. It being fully understood that those mediums who attract the lesser developed order of spirits are, themselves, in the earlier stages of incarnation, whatever their temporary earthly conditions or surroundings may appear to be; while those attracting the higher class of spirits are, themselves, further along in the series of earthly embodiments which are necessary for the completion of life's purposes.

The spirit having gained all that is possible by direct and indirect association with matter, will immediately pass on into its stages of spiritual life, which it is not the province of this work to deal with. In short, there is a purpose in everything; though veiled, it may be, from human understanding, it can be explained as outworking a result which, in its finality, has but good for its aim and end.

Through the law of re-incarnation the justice of heaven is made manifest, and one human being has, in time and eternity, an opportunity of realizing just as much of good fortune and of bad fortune, of sunshine and shadow, as has every other individual. It is impossible to more than indicate what we mean. Volumes might be written, but it is our purpose to awaken thoughts which the development of ages will serve to stimulate.

PART XVII.

SUGGESTIVE THOUGHTS.

SUGGESTIVE THOUGHTS.

(Entered according to Act of Congress, in the year 1893, by AUGUSTA W. FLETCHER, M. D., in the office of the Librarian of Congress at Washington.)

Beware of conclusions.
There are no finalities.
Work is the consoler of many sorrows.
Ignorance is the twin-sister of wickedness.
A thing done in secret is done all the same.
Creeds are the monuments of man's stupidity.
Knowledge is the only stepping-stone to power.
He is, indeed, weak who finds all humanity frail.
No man is strong enough to walk absolutely alone.
Unkind words are often regretted; kind words never.
Heaven and hell are states of development, not localities.

Thought is a tangible expression of the desire of the spirit.

Man has not to fear the devils without, but within himself.

He who remembers his own grief adds to the sorrow of others.

Restitution is better than repentance, since it includes both.

Death is the passing from a lower to a higher stage of existence.

In searching for the faults of others you may fail to find your own.

Learn to creep well, for upon it your walking depends.

The strong man is he who finds the most to depend upon in others.

Reputation is like thin ice, serviceable until you wish to stand upon it.

Hate inflicts no wound so great as that which falls upon its possessor.

Act according to your conscience and leave the consequences to God.

To conquer self, and eliminate evil tendencies, are the real purposes of life.

Be happy yourself and you will be able to conquer the sadness of others.

Education, in the true sense of the word, is another name for experience.

No man should judge another until he knows him, then he won't need to.

Justify your action to yourself, and, in time, its justice will be recognized.

The respect of the world is a blessing; the respect of one's self is a greater one.

Woman's forgiveness of woman accords with the capacity of her affection.

Thoughts are great not so much in what they teach, as in what they suggest.

Hope is the voice of the spirit speaking within the silence of the human heart.

Life after death is dependent upon life before death, progress being a universal law.

No religion can be said to be of God unless it be universal in its application and result.

Expect no greater excellence in others, than that which thou art prepared to offer.

The truly polite are the truly kind. Good manners are one thing, true politeness another.

The understanding of books is important; but the understanding of humanity is more so.

No soul is lost by going down to hell to drag another out; but gains, instead, an added glory.

He, indeed, is in a fool's paradise who is satisfied with the small pleasures that ignorance affords.

What the highest has attained, is possible to the lowest, time and eternity working out the result.

All things existing are but the representation of a thought expressed; thus thought becomes a reality.

Justice, love and fidelity are the attributes of God; and as a man is possessed of these, so is he God-like.

Every man must become a ruler over himself before he is able to enter in upon any degree of real happiness.

All things that are possible are possible to God; yet He is governed by the impossible, as are his subjects.

Live each day as if it was your last on earth, remembering, however, that unborn eternities are before you.

Sin is a form of disease which the undeveloped are susceptible to in their passage from a lower to a higher state.

Thinking evil is, in reality, one degree worse than doing it, since, without thought, evil would not be committed.

The body is the temple of the spirit. The spirit is the expression which the soul makes in its contact with matter.

It is not what people have been, but what they are, that should form the basis of your acquaintance and judgment.

Thinking is the activity of the spirit which, reflecting itself upon the different parts of the brain, produces a given result.

The good are not found among those who have never sinned, but rather among those who have conquered and overcome sin.

Play well thy part, and yet, play not that part too well; for in the perfection of thine acting thine object may stand forth revealed.

Begin each day with the determination of conquering the evils of yesterday, and find the good which has seemingly been overlooked.

Prayer, when relating to spiritual attainments, is the voice of the spirit; but when relating to earthly desires becomes the soul of selfishness.

There is no logic whereby evil shall be done that good may come, for in the spirit of things it is the cause, and not the result, which is important.

No man has the right to ask for any blessing that he is not willing to do his utmost to obtain for others, and only then, does he become worthy of it.

The sun is always shining; it is only the clouds that obscure its light. The spirit is always in the light, but the desires of the body obscure its rays.

Those who desire to be truly happy must first be in harmony with themselves, which, in turn, will bring them into harmonious relationship with others.

Any person desiring goodness, can, by thinking goodly

thoughts, place himself in direct relationship with the soul of all good, and, thereby, obtain his desire.

The developed man or woman is responsive to every condition of human life, since development consists in conquering and overcoming all lower conditions.

Theology is one thing, religion another; theologies change with the requirements of the times; religion is of God, and is the same yesterday, to-day and forever.

Goodness is the only positive quality in the world. Evil exists only negatively. All truly wise men are truly good, for wisdom and goodness move in the same orbit.

When man has comprehended himself, he has found the key to the universe. Everything that is possible to the world, as a world, man holds within his own organization.

While the commission of a sinful act can never be blotted out of life's book, the result of that act, by earnest endeavor, may be made the stepping-stone to great good.

Many who are educated in the schools know nothing of life and its responsibilities; many who have no education at all, are able to comprehend and rightly use the laws of life.

Nature is but one grand expression of the thoughts of God; those who are at war with nature are at war with God; those who are at peace with nature are at peace with God.

In remembering the fatherhood of God, and the motherhood of nature, forget not the brotherhood of man, for if that be remembered, the other two follow in natural sequence.

When the world has recognized the law of absolute justice for all, charity will no longer be needed for the unfortunate, since it is the divine intention that all should be alike blessed.

Death is the separation of the spirit from contact with coarser material elements; but the spirit will have a body of a more refined nature, corresponding to that earthly one which it formerly inhabited.

He who seeks to deceive himself plays the part of a fool; while he who seeks to deceive others is more of a villain than a fool. For deception and hypocrisy there is no excuse; they are, however, the methods employed by cowards.

There is no forgiveness of sin either in this world or the next; salvation comes only when the sin is conquered and overcome, since, like a sword-cut, it is bound to leave its scar. Sins are like open sores, and goodness is the only ointment that will heal them.

The aristocracy of blood rules Europe, while the aristocracy of money rules America; but the aristocracy of character is recognized in all lands and all worlds. The first two are the result of circumstances external to the individual, the third, however, comes as the crowning glory of interior development, and, instead of being dropped at the doorway of the grave, crosses the threshold and becomes a recognized glory in the world beyond.

www.ingramcontent.com/pod-product-compliance
Lightning Source LLC
Chambersburg PA
CBHW031936230426

43672CB00010B/1936